CHALICE OF THE DOVE

By Gillian DeArmond

AMERICA WEST PUBLISHERS

Library of Congress Cataloging-in-Publication Data

DeArmond, Gillian, 1937-
     Chalice Of The Dove by Gillian DeArmond.

     ISBN 0-992356-94-7 : $12.95

First Edition Printed by
AMERICA WEST PUBLISHERS
P.O. BOX 3300
BOZEMAN, MT 59772

Printed in the United States of America
10 9 8 7 6 5 4 3 2 1

Contents

CHALICE OF THE DOVE

CHALICE OF THE DOVE

This Book
is dedicated
to Time Travelers
everywhere.

INTRODUCTION

When responding to the questons set forth in the following pages I am sharing the information given to me by Spirit over the years. In one or two cases I am expressing a personal opinion, and so specify . You are not being asked to believe that which I have written. As always, we must each search for and find our own truth. If this writing serves any purpose at all then let it serve to share ideas and concepts for you to consider at your leisure.

"My Doctrine is not mine, but His who sent me"
— John 7:16

POEM

A darling Soul the Divine Spark creates
To come in wonder to a world unknown.
Returning home these wonders it relates
And many times will open new eyes again.

And with each awakening
The soul a forward step must take
Towards the arms of its Creator
If the final transition it is to make.

And in that moment when time stands still
Before the stars burst forth anew
Then all free souls will rise on high;
The new Creators, blessed few.

And when the world is born again
And that first sun rises on sights unseen
Then will souls their flesh regain
To stand once more in pastures green.

ONE

Question: WHO OR WHAT AM I?

Gillian: You are a sentient being produced by the combination of light and intelligence. Your original form is the **diamond form** of perfect light. In the beginning, the Creator imbued your original form with the spark of Divine Intelligence, the essence of your soul. You are ancient and yet you are a child experiencing the first stages of your evolution through the three dimensional realities, manifesting on the mental, emotional, physical and spiritual planes. You hold the potential of immortality within your own soul. Only you can ignite the living spark of the Three Fold Flame; power, wisdom and love within.

Since the material I have received about the Diamond Form is voluminous and being formated into a book itself, I will offer a brief explanation. Let us look at "forms": (See diagram on following page.) For practical purposes they may be divided into two groups; *Original Form* and *Form in Use*. Original Form may be described as a diamond with an unknown number of facets, having a positive and negative polarity and containing a vibratory frequency which carries all the potential of the **Source** together with the specific frequency which individualizes this particular *Diamond* as *You*. The first frequency, being an eminence from the Source—and therefore incorruptible—is the **soul essence** and cannot be destroyed, but will always return to the point of origin. The additional "you" frequency, through manifest experience in many forms, times and places and on many levels will either enhance the original essence, in which case it will be fit to blend *and become a part of the first essence, thereby, returning to the Source*, or it will be so corrupted (dark) as to be incapable of union with the light and must, therefore, be discarded. What is so nice about this whole system is that it is not a matter of luck but of **choice**—*our choice.* There is no magic, there is only knowledge through understanding expressed as unconditional love and if you do not understand unconditional love you understand nothing.

Forms in Use, of course refers to whatever form our original energy may be working through at the time. We may, for example, be experiencing the lessons of homo sapiens on planet earth, or perhaps we have danced a merry jig in the Pleiades, or studied science on Orion, or used our finer energy forms to visit our galaxy, or teach from the astral plane. We may have flown with the eagle and swum with the dolphin. There are, indeed, more possibilities in heaven and earth than most of us have dreamed of, but remember, *if you can dream it, then it is within the realm of your possibilities.*

Perhaps the most valuable purpose served by the physical body is that during an incarnation this **physical form** creates for us an **artificial separation** from all those around us. In so doing it affords us the optimum opportunity for the exercise of free-will. For it is by our own choice that we progress immortally.

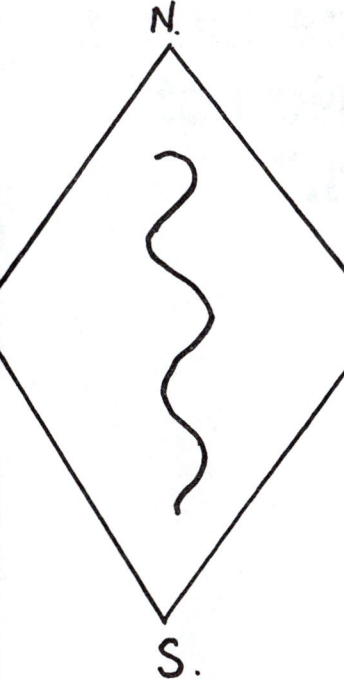

N.

S.

THE "DIAMOND FORM", ORIGINAL
FORM WITH A NORTH/SOUTH
POLARITY RELATIVE TO THE
SOURCE AND WITH AN
1 D SINE WAVE FROM THE
UPPER TO THE LOWER
SPATIAL MID·POINT

"Space and Time exist in
the Infinite Now of
Creation."

Two

Q: WHAT IS OUR PLACE IN THE COSMOS?

G: We may think of it in this way; in the beginning God dreamed the creation, and the totality of God's dream is the Law of One. Then, harnessing the properties of light, He made his creation manifest on many dimensions. These dimensions, once made manifest, become subject to the Laws of Nature and Physics. We are experiencing in the three dimensional level of His creation and our responsibility—our place if you like—is the stewardship of creation.

God created man as a sentient being, a true aspect of Himself containing His potential, that in time, man may become a co-creator with God. So one might say that man's place in creation is this; that man is God's representative within the Creation and his duty to God is the care of God's creation and the development of his own soul. On the day when a human perfects his own soul, he too will understand the energies of light. On that day he will truly become a co-creator.

"Life is Truth and the Truth is Life."

THREE

Q: **H**OW DOES THE HUMAN BEING ON EARTH FIT IN AND WHAT IS OUR CONNECTION TO THE EARTH?

G: Earth is part of a whole three dimensional creation which in itself has many planes or levels of experience. Earth is the first level of our experiences as physically embodied beings within the three dimensional creation. We have Elder Brothers manifesting higher levels of physical embodiment elsewhere in the galaxy on planes of existence akin to our own. Man evolves through more than one physical plane before changing into a spiritually manifest being and he may spend millennia on each plane of experience.

Like earth, we are part of the Creation. We are no more or less important than all life which exists, including the earth. In the physical expression of the Creation, it would serve us well to remember that the earth can exist without us, but we cannot exist here three-dimensionally without earth. We have that responsibility, therefore, to maintain, to nurture and to live in harmony with the planet.

"Personal Power is in direct proportion to the integrity of the soul."

FOUR

Q: IS THERE AN EVOLUTION OF CONSCIOUSNESS IN THE SENTIENT BEING, OR DOES THE SENTIENT BEING HAVE THE KNOWLEDGE AND IS SIMPLY AWAKENING THAT KNOWLEDGE FROM THE CREATOR?

G: In order to understand the question we have to look at the process. It is true to say that once the being is made sentient within the creation, then it is an evolving being, but the essence within must also be considered. To do this we must ask the question, *"What is the soul?"* The soul is like the pearl in the oyster. The Soul Essence is like the piece of sand that gets into the oyster and becomes a nucleus around which the oyster creates the pearl. The sand irritates the oyster and the oyster diverts its energy into coating the piece of sand and so creates a pearl. In this way the soul of the individual contains, both the Essence which the Creator placed there, and the Pearl which the individual has created through his experiences from lifetime to lifetime. Each lifetime experience is like an aggravation which triggers reaction in the oyster and affords opportunity for growth. That is why we often say that we learn more from our difficulties than from the "good" things which happen to us. This is because it is the annoyances and difficulties that tend to trigger us to think about who we are, what we are doing and where we are going. In that process we add energy around the essence of the soul which the Creator gave to us in the beginning.

At any point in our evolution we contain at the core of our soul the perfect essence that our Creator gave to us to work with in the first place, together with all that we have ever learned and accomplished since that time. You may have shined your soul in such a way that you have created a beautiful pearl and are an illuminated and enlightened being. Or you may have made many discordant choices. You may have responded very negatively, lifetime after lifetime, to all the prods and probes that were intended to move you forward. In that process you may have created something very unpleasant and not at all pearl-like. Spirit once said to me, *"Personal power is in direct proportion to the integrity of your soul".* Power is energy and if we would have energy to share with others, we must first look to the shining of our own souls and the creation of our own illumined pearl.

FIVE

Q: Does every one have an immortal soul?

G: Every one has the *potential* for immortality. Unless you choose, throughout a cycle of incarnations, to ignite the living spark within your own soul you will not achieve immortality. Christ Himself said, *"...He that heareth my word, and believeth on Him that sent me, hath everlasting life..."* — John 5:24. That statement has an equal and opposite statement which says, *"Therefore, those who do not understand, believe or follow the teachings which He gave will not achieve immortality"*. We clarify that here by adding that although Jesus the Nazarene was the only *well documented* being ever to come down and manifest within human form the *full* potential of the Godhead, so that we could all observe a living demonstration of immortality, nonetheless, the teachings that he brought have been given many times by many great teachers from the far, far past—Mohammed, Buddha, Confucius etc.—up to modern day teachers.[1] So it is erroneous to think that only those who are "Christians" will be saved. This is inaccurate. It is *all* those who follow the teachings of Christ, although individually they may have received those teachings from an entirely different source.

---

[1] Christians in general refer to Christ as *"The only begotten Son of God"*. The key word here is "begotten". Considering that each soul contains the Essence of the Creator making each one of us a son or daughter of God the use of the word "begotten" indicates to us that some special and different process was involved in the conception of Jesus Christ.

Your Notes

Six

Q: DESCRIBE THE "SELVES" WE HAVE, CONSCIOUS, SUBCONSCIOUS AND SUPERCONSCIOUS AND THE EVOLUTION OF CONSCIOUSNESS IN AN EVOLVING SOUL.

G: It is the conscious thinking mind supported by the subconscious awareness that maintain the ego of the personality during our lifetimes. That which is referred to as the superconsiousness is also sometimes known as the Higher Self. There is often confusion using the word "consciousness", which itself overlaps between the spiritual and the physical being. Therefore, I would say that the conscious and the subconscious minds are directly related to the three dimensional expression of ourselves through our personality. While the superconsciousness or "higher" consciousness is the storage of that knowledge and experience which more properly belongs to our immortal selves in spirit.

In addition when I refer to the terms "soul" and "spirit" I would say that the spirit is the energy of the soul in action.

"Each Dimension expresses itself in Multiple levels of frequency. The third dimension in which we exist has twenty-two planes of experience."

SEVEN

Q: How long is a cycle of incarnations? How long do we actually have to ignite that spark of immortality within ourselves?

G: From the information I have received from Spirit, the cycles of evolution last approximately 50,000 years. Every 50,000 years a new generation arises for the experience of humanity as it evolves. So we may have experienced a 50,000 cycle which included Lumeria and another 50,000 year cycle with the Atlantean, and then another 50,000 year cycle with the present incarnation. And it goes back to the beginnings and will continue until the "end". It also seems that at the end of every 50,000 year cycle, there is a period of evaluation or judgment by "higher authority", which will determine which souls have the right— have earned the privilege—of continuing their progress, and which souls have done little but dissipate the energy of which they are made. I am not so much making a statement of "right" and "wrong" here, as a statement about the nature of energy. Energy is never lost, it changes. If you, in the process of evolving your soul, have generated positive energy, have converted that energy which you have to work with into love and humility—into virtue—then you have increased your own energetic field. You have thus increased your personal power.

Let us more carefully examine the statement from Spirit which I mentioned earlier, *"Your personal power is in direct proportion to the integrity of your own soul"*. By power, they were referencing the amount or quantity of energy which is directly under your control from lifetime to lifetime. If, throughout many lifetimes, you have only wasted the energy you have, and only misused that energy in some way, then at the end of a cycle of lifetimes, there will be no energy over which you have control and that you can use to propel yourself forward into the next cycle. You will have lost yourself. You will have wasted yourself.

The Immortal Essence of your soul does not belong to you. It belongs always to the Creator. If you should be unfortunate enough to have no energy left because you have wasted it all, and all that there is the essence of your soul, that essence will return to the Creator and you as an individual entity will cease to exist.

Eight

Q: Where are we at this time within the current 50,000 year cycle?

G: At this time we are very quickly approaching the end of this cycle. My understanding is that the completion of this cycle is in the year 2026. So for most of us on the planet now, there is a very short space of time left to us...but it is long enough. One minute is time enough if you understand energy, because it is only the physical manifest form which is confined within linear time. Beyond the manifest form, time does not exist as we know it. So there is always time *enough*. But it requires that you become awake—that you become a living, conscious human being. To be awake means to be aware of your potential and aware of what it requires to move forward toward that potential. The minimum requirement is the lighting of your own spark to ignite the eternal Three-Fold Flame of the soul. (See page 185 on "Earth Changes").

"The 22nd plane is both the inner and the outer — the place of Golden Light which is the beginning and the end of this creation."

NINE

Q: So what is our purpose as human beings evolving ourselves?

G. That we are evolving back to our beginnings. Remember that our beginning is the perfect essence of the Creator containing all potential at the heart of our souls. Again, going back to the analogy of the pearl; we need to look first at the ways in which we are living. We are living physically, emotionally, mentally and spiritually in any incarnation. Those are the four planes on which we are made manifest. All lives are therefore physical, emotional, mental and spiritual lives. The reactions in the physical reality tend to be based more in the emotional body than in the other three. That is to say our reactions mostly come as an emotional response to any given situation.

Now let us imagine that we are looking back to our very first lifetime. Before coming into incarnation, the Creator may have said to us, *"Here you are, an individual soul, a sentient being and here is the whole of Creation, go and enjoy it and be happy."* But to the contrary, our experience of the physical reality was not a happy one. We endured pain and suffering and hardship. So we left that lifetime with a lot of negative perspective and a lot of emotional attachment to that negativity. The emotional attachment guarantees that we will have another incarnation because we will want to come back to the planet and remedy our emotional state. We will want to bring it back into balance.

So we come back and we have another lifetime. And we may have had a very "good" life. But this time we may have become extremely emotionally attached by *human* love to one or more other people we knew on the planet. That experience of emotional love ties us once again to the round of reincarnation in the three dimensional reality. **It is the emotional attachments that bind us to the cycle of reincarnation and keep bringing us back again and again.**

This is not our purpose. Our purpose is not forever to be reincarnated on this planet: Our purpose is to be evolving back into our origins of pure spirit, pure essence. Our goal is our soul's perfection. And what is a perfect soul? It is that state of being wherein the soul has detached itself from all purposes of self and is free to join in union with the Creator and so fulfill, not its own, but the Creator's purposes.

So when one is asking what is our purpose as human beings on this planet: Our purpose is to fulfill that which the Creator intended for us. Namely to be a manifest aspect of Himself caring for His creation. That really is the underlying driving need for humans. And the only way we can achieve that is if our goal, our only goal, is achieving our own soul's perfection. This is because it is our soul's perfection which is required of us in order to return to our beginnings and truly reflect our Creator. We are acting as reflectors of the Creator. If you looked into the mirror, what you would see would be a reflection of yourself and that reflection shows you taking action as an expression of your own free-will. In the same way every living soul is a reflection of some aspect of Creator, and is taking action in behalf of the Creator within the creation. So if you have any goal other than your soul's perfection, you are not going to be able to accurately reflect the Creator. You are reflecting a distortion of the Creator, not the true essence that was originally given to you.

As you go from lifetime to lifetime you build more and more emotional ties with people and situations and emotions on the planet. Whether it is this planet, or any other planet the truth is the same. You are becoming more attached to the manifestation, which is the mirror image, and less attached to the Source Itself, which is the Creator, and in so doing you are creating a separation between yourself and your Source.

So when we are addressing the question of what should be *Someone's Purpose*, just set the goal as *the perfection of your own soul* and you will realize that *you* can have no purpose. Because every purpose that *you* think of, every purpose that *you* have, is a human purpose and not necessarily God's purpose. When you have perfected your soul, this moves you into unity with Divine Mind. When you are united with Divine Mind, then you are a true reflection of the Creator and all the purposes you have will become God's purposes.

"The pattern of life is the double helix and the motion of life is the convoluted curve."

Ten

Q: Is there any real way to measure our own spiritual progress?

G: No, there is not. We can evaluate our actions. But even in order to evaluate the actions of our lives, we have to learn the art of viewing things objectively not subjectively. The natural way for the human to view things is subjectively. Everyone sees things from their own point of view.

In order to truly begin examining our own soul, we need to develop the art of viewing objectively, from the outside point of view, not the inside point of view. In reality it is not even necessary for you to evaluate your spiritual progress at all, because when we are doing that which is appropriate for our soul's growth, our spiritual evolution will be automatic. As your soul grows so your awareness level will increase and, more and more, your actions and automatic responses will reflect the God-Source within you. As time passes you will arrive at different points in your life when you will just have the realization that you are doing something "right"—that you are making some progress.

Your Notes

Eleven

Q: ARE "SELF-MASTERY" AND "PERFECTING ONE'S OWN SOUL" TWO DIFFERENT CONCEPTS?

G: Yes. Self-mastery is an appropriate step for us to take *towards* the perfection of our souls. And yet, it may be that your way toward soul perfection in a particular lifetime requires that you are incapable of self-mastery. For example, the paralyzed individual may not have "mastery" over the physical aspect of his or her manifestation, and yet the very condition he is in may well be aiding in the advancement towards the perfection of his soul. Self mastery is a tool on the road to our spiritual perfection. But always we are brought to points of choosing. Once we have achieved self-mastery, we find we are at a point of great choosing, for it is from this pinnacle of achievement that we elect to service our ego and "rule in the world", or we come to realize the worthlessness of our own efforts and abandon ourselves to God.

In working toward self-mastery, the simplest way I know of is to walk the Four-Fold Path which we discuss in depth on page 33. Whatever path one chooses, the most important thing to remember is to walk our path with objective truth and honesty.

Our natural view of the circumstances we find ourselves in is always subjective. And isn't it true that we can justify almost anything that we chose to do? The pathway of objective honesty allows for no justification and no excuses, only acceptance. Acceptance of ourselves and others with love and humility. And it is this development of love and humility within ourselves that leads to the attainment of self-mastery.

Before we begin to harness the power of our higher selves, we must first have control of this being which expresses our immortal soul on the three-dimensional plane. We must therefore, take charge of ourselves on all physical levels. We must accept responsibility for and become fully conscious of all our thoughts, words and deeds. Once we have attained conscious awareness of all our acts in the three dimensional plane, we are then ready to proceed to the expansion of ourselves on the spiritual planes.

The perfection of the soul is a paradox. On the one hand, all that we should be reaching toward is the goal of our perfection, even as Christ admonished the disciples to "be perfect." And yet, if *all* we do is chosen to add to the glory of *our* souls alone, then our works accomplish less than nothing. Instead, we must choose to do our work for the love of doing it and pray in all humility that God will place before us that work which is most appropriate for our soul's journey.

TWELVE

Q: WILL YOU EXPLAIN WHAT DETACHMENT IS AND WHY IT IS IMPORTANT FOR THE PERFECTION OF ONE'S SOUL?

G: This is part of what I was saying in learning to view objectively, because from the objective view you are detached from the subjective view. Total detachment has to be a process that is used if you are ever going to journey on the road to perfecting your own soul. The attachments that we have, whether they are mental, physical, emotional or spiritual, are all subjective. Attachments to the world that we live in to the relationships and situations which we are involved in. Very often we are most attached to our knowledge, to what we believe we know and understand.

Unconditional love, the Creator's kind of love, is founded in compassion and compassion has no emotion in it. To love unconditionally is to love all things equally and without judgement. If we are ever going to learn to love in that way, then we have to be attached to no single thing. Because as soon as you have attachment to something or someone then you cannot be loving equally.

Christ said, *"Love ye one another as I have loved you."* John 5:22-27. He loved all equally. He loved the taxpayer and the prostitute, the scribes and the pharisees all equally. That is not to say that you agree with what that person is doing, but rather that you recognize that the original essence of the Creator is within. And it is this which you love. It is the original essence which you love and honor in every single thing which crosses your path, both in nature and in people.

How can you say, *"I love my thumb more than I love my little finger?"* Don't you love them equally? It might be true that if you had one of them amputated for some reason you would make the evaluation that you would be better off without your little finger than without your thumb. So you would chose to let go of your little finger rather than let go of your thumb. But that's got nothing to do with you having equal care for both your thumb and your little finger. Attachment to any *one* thing prevents unconditional love of *all* things.

Perhaps the biggest holdup in our progress towards detachment is our attachment to our knowledge and our spiritual beliefs. For example, you will find well-intentioned people who are wholly attached to a concept of having a spiritual center and doing good work which occupies their thinking twenty-four hours a day believing they are practicing unconditional love. How can they be practicing unconditional love when they are wholly attached to the advancement of their center and its ideas? Even when their desire for a spiritual center is to help people and it came out of a genuine feeling of love and compassion, it is still a human feeling attached to their human judgements of what other people need. I can't count the times I have heard people say, *"I see my service to humanity as helping to raise consciousness".* This is an example of attachment to ego. We must ask where such a person believes their level of spiritual evolution to be when they feel that they are both capable and worthy to go out and raise other people's consciousness. How, I wonder, do they make the evaluation of their own consciousness? On what basis? Who came and told them that they were illuminated beings, that they were capable of raising other people's consciousness? When you do meet a truly illumined being, you find that they are not telling anyone else how to live. People may ask them for help and advise, but they are not out there telling them.

The shining light of all who practice unconditional love is a deep and sincere humility. Remember John the Baptist? Despite his many followers, he considered himself unfit to unlatch Christ's sandals. If we can detach from all things including *our desire* to do anything, including "good" deeds, then we are a tool in readiness for the hand of God. He may not want us to open spiritual centers, or do "great" deeds, but whatever God asks of us, we will do for the joy of doing in alignment with His will. In order to serve the will of God, we must detach from the expression of our own will.

"To enter a Black Hole is to exit into the light of a new plane."

Thirteen

Q: CAN ONE FEEL CARE, CONCERN AND UNCONDITIONAL LOVE FOR OTHERS (INCLUDING MARRIAGE PARTNERS) AND STILL MAINTAIN EMOTIONAL DETACHMENT?

G: Absolutely. Our care and concern for others coming out of unconditional love is founded in compassion and compassion has no emotion in it. The emotions of this body are only of the three-dimensional experience. Compassion, on the other hand, is founded in pure spirit. So we certainly can, and hopefully will, feel care and concern for all others and yet we will have no emotional attachment to the situation. This is a matter of giving unconditional love for *no purpose*, only joining in the creative force of love which is equally offered to all living things.

When we are emotionally attached, we have expectations and anticipations of behavior from that other person. When you are looking at your mate or marriage partner and loving them unconditionally then, yes, you can be emotionally *detached* from them. For when you are more concerned with the happiness of your partner than with the happiness of yourself, then you are loving unconditionally. And if your concern is for their happiness, then you will not emotionally attach yourself to them in such a way that your attachment to them may prevent them from fulfilling what they perceive as their happiness.

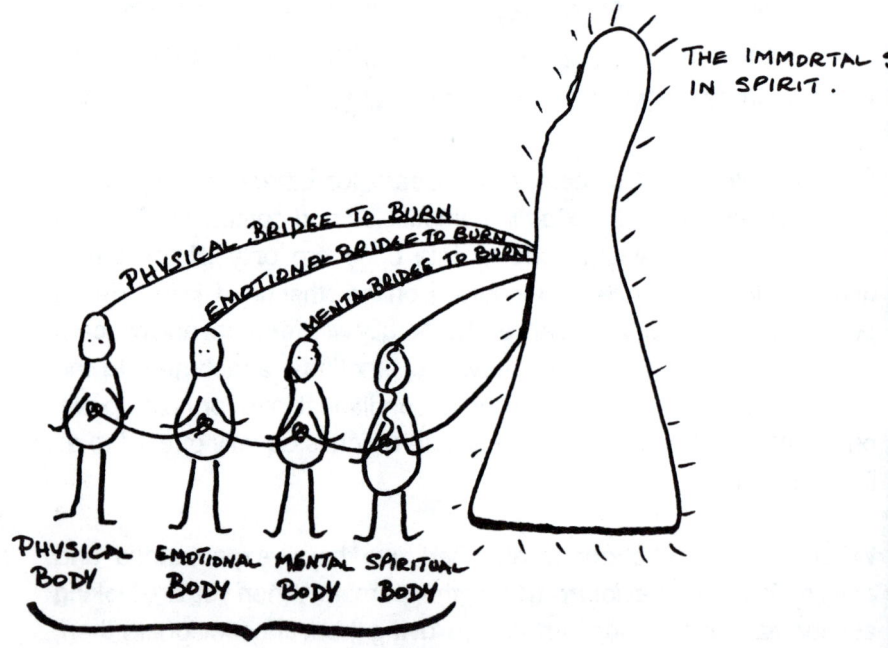

THE IMMORTAL S̶
IN SPIRIT.

PHYSICAL BRIDGE TO BURN
EMOTIONAL BRIDGE TO BURN
MENTAL BRIDGE TO BURN

PHYSICAL
BODY

EMOTIONAL
BODY

MENTAL
BODY

SPIRITUAL
BODY

THE 4 PLANES OF MANIFESTATION

FOURTEEN

Q: IS THERE A PATH WE CAN WALK WHICH WILL ENABLE US TO HAVE CLARITY AND UNDERSTANDING IN THE MATTER OF OUR SOUL'S PROGRESS?

G: Yes, you can walk *The Four-Fold Path* to enlightenment. The Four-Fold Path moves us through that level of conscious awareness of all our actions which lead to self-mastery. It is the simplest way I know to progress yourself toward your spiritual evolution. It is the pathway by which you may detach yourself from the material world whilst you are still living in the material world. It is the path by which you may attain that level of consciousness expressed by Christ in the statement, *"Be in the world, but not of the world"*.

If you will look at the drawing on the facing page you will see that we have pictorially expressed the immortal self in spirit, connected to the self that you know, expressing on the three-dimensional plane with a physical body, an emotional body, a mental body and a spiritual body. As you can see, each of those bodies is connected by a bridge directly to your immortal spiritual being and each body is also tied to the next body.

The process is very simple. We first must understand that it is the emotions and the emotional body which tie us to the constant round of reincarnation on this planet. The Four-Fold Path is a process of detaching ourselves emotionally from all the things which exist in our lives here on planet Earth.

Begin with the physical being. Examine all the physical things in your life to which you are attached and slowly detach yourself from them, one by one. This is not to say that you cannot have the material things of this life. It is simply to say that you must not be emotionally tied to them. For example, there is nothing wrong with having wealth. But there is something intrinsically missing from that of point of view which is more concerned with wealth than with spirit. So it is a case of where your focus and attention lie.

Proceed, then, with the examination and detachment of yourself on the physical level Step by step detach yourself from all those things which tie you to the physical plane. Once you have achieved this, imagine that you are now burning the "bridge" which connects your physical being to your immortal spiritual self.

Now begin the process of detachment at the emotional level. Examine all your emotional feelings, ties and connections, and transmute all of them into unconditional love, rather than the conditional love of the personality. The road to unconditional love is really a process of neutralization of your emotional energy, bringing earthly love, hate, anger, sorrow, joy all to a place of calm. Once you have achieved this emotional detachment with an equal love for all things, without focus in one particular direction, then you can detach your emotional body by burning that "bridge" which connects it to the spiritual.

Having done this you now move on to the mental body. It is detachment at the mental level which is so difficult for most of us simply because we perceive ourselves by that which we know. *"I know physics, therefore I am of some importance"*. Detachment from our knowledge, detachment from all that we know is the hardest thing to do for most of us. Because it is letting go of this knowledge which reduces us to the *nothingness and humility* of the soul which we are trying to achieve. Once you have detached yourself mentally, then burn the "bridge" of the mental body. You will see now if you will look at the diagram again, that once those three bridges are burned, the only connection you now have on the physical plane is directly through your spiritual being from your immortal aspect. In this way all the actions, thoughts, words and deeds of the physical, emotional and mental bodies will be directed by your inner self through Spirit. This is the Four-Fold Path. This is the process which leads you to self-mastery and connects you on all levels with Spirit at all times.

"To Journey to the stars is to follow the spirals."

FIFTEEN

Q: WHEN YOU SPEAK OF OUR "NOTHINGNESS", DO YOU MEAN THAT EACH INDIVIDUAL HAS NO VALUE?

G: No. Every single living soul is of great value. The living soul is the most important thing in the universe. As Spirit once explained to me, *"Could you imagine the opening of Beethoven's fifth symphony with one of the notes missing?"* Life, all life is like a great symphony and every single note is important, for if one of the notes were missing, then the harmony would be lost.

When I refer to our *nothingness*, I speak of that place of self-awareness which each soul must seek and find for itself. For myself, when I look at the wickedness of my life, it is like a dark shadow which shames me. And when I look at that which I perceive as the goodness of my life and compare it with all the gifts that Spirit has given me throughout the years, my goodness is a pitifully small heap which humbles me before my Lord. In making those comparisons, I have no difficulty in finding my place in *nothingness*.

Again speaking only for myself, I do not attempt to collect those things I perceive as "good" and offer them to God, saying, *"Lord this is what I have done which is good. Please judge me on this."* Instead, I pray that God will never judge me at all and I only abandon myself to His love and mercy and hope that my Judgment will be overlooked. It is true God said he would save a city if He could find one good man. Maybe when the time comes, God out of love and charity, may find one good act in my life that may save me. But as I said, it is not His *judgment* that I count on, but His *mercy*.

"You are the keeper of your flame."

Sixteen

Q: At what point does one actually become a giver of light, instead a taker of light?

G: The Four-Fold Path is the foundation, the path that you can walk in your normal life, while interacting with the world around you and develop the art of, *"Being in the world, but not of the world."* Once you have achieved this then you are ready to bring all things into balance in your life. The point of perfect balance is expressed in the Maltese cross which you can see on page 40. As you will see the Maltese cross is formed of four triangles with their points touching at the center. And here it is depicted with a rose at the center. The rose represents your immortal soul. The four triangles represent the four planes of manifestation on this planet. When you have walked those four planes into perfect balance and harmony with your existence, you can then hold up those four triangles like a flower closing. This you see in the next drawing, page 41. That next drawing is the lower half of the pyramid, which is the lower half of your original form of your *diamond form.* So once you have walked the *Four-Fold Path* and detached yourself, you can then bring all four levels into perfect balance. Once that balance is achieved the energy then is enfolded around your soul, and you have recreated the basis of your original form. At that point you have achieved Christ Consciousness. You have achieved that perfect balance within yourself. You then become an emitter of light. You are then connected with your own immortality.

THE MEANING OF THE FOUR-ARMED CROSS:—
THE 3-FOLD FLAME MUST BE FULLY ACTIVATED
AND REFLECTING ON ALL FOUR PLANES, THEN
THE FOUR "SIDES" CAN UNITE AND YOUR PYRAMID
OF PERSONAL POWER IS FORMED WITH YOUR SOUL
AS THE CAPSTONE. IT IS WITHIN THIS PYRAMID
THAT YOU CAN CREATE THE ENERGY TO LEAP
THE ABYSS INTO ETERNITY.

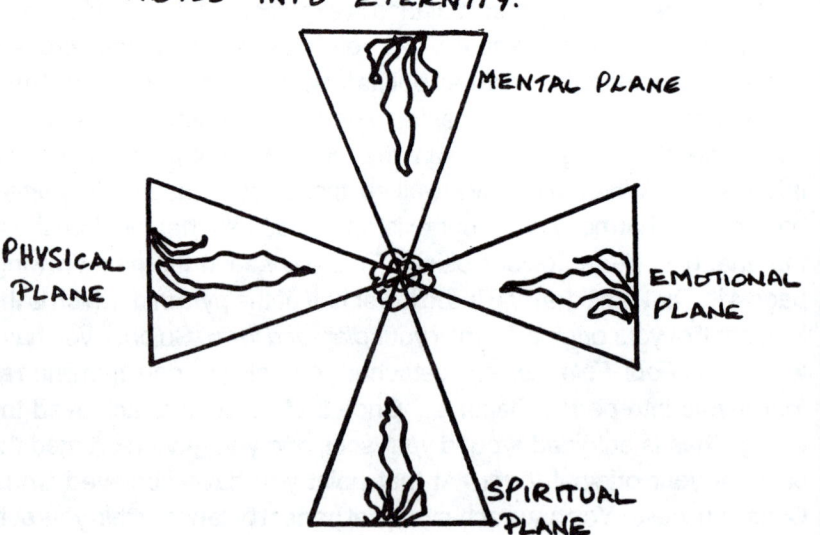

LOWER, OR MANIFESTING ASPECT, OF YOUR
ORIGINAL DIAMOND FORM OF LIGHT.

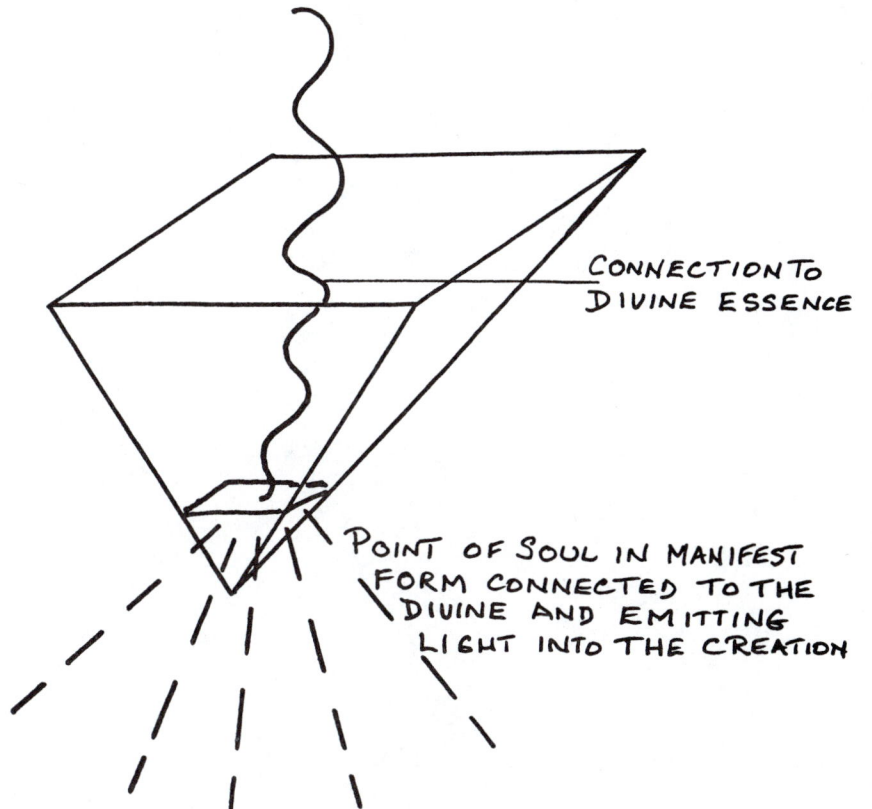

CONNECTION TO
DIVINE ESSENCE

POINT OF SOUL IN MANIFEST
FORM CONNECTED TO THE
DIVINE AND EMITTING
LIGHT INTO THE CREATION

Your Notes

SEVENTEEN

Q: SPEAK ABOUT THE TERM "LIGHT WORKERS" EXPRESSED BY MANY TO DESCRIBE THEMSELVES. MANY CALL THEMSELVES "LIGHT WORKERS" BELIEVING THEY ARE HERE ON THE PLANET TO GIVE LIGHT FROM THE CREATOR.

G: I would like to think that all those who make that statement truly are so perfectly evolved that they do nothing but give light. And I dare say that there are beings on the planet today who are creatures of pure light, who shed light wherever they go. I also think it is fair to say that there are *degrees* of light, in the same way that you can light one small candle, or you can light a 500 watt bulb. So for every degree of perfection that we achieve, from that level we may be shedding light. And I also think it is fair to say, that those who are giving the most light to this dark planet, are also those who are the least likely to be saying anything about it.

We can, however, investigate the possibility of an entirely different meaning in this statement "light workers". There are people who sincerely believe that they came from other planets, possibly arriving here by the processes known as "Walking-In" or "UFOs". These people have the capability of literally working with light within the laws of Physics. I don't discount this possibility at all. It has been my experience that there are beings from more evolved dimensions, who at this time of transition are directly communicating with humans, and through humans, for the explicit purpose of bringing additional light particles into the physical, mental and emotional structures of the people on this planet.

So when we are talking about the purely divine light of God going through someone because their soul has been perfected, that is one thing. But in addition to that, I think it is accurate to say that there are other beings who are working with light in particle form, imbuing it into our consciousness. It may well be that many who refer to themselves as "light workers" on this planet are directly involved with those beings from elsewhere in the cosmos.

Eighteen

Q: Please speak about the most important universal laws for human beings to live by and why.

G: There are two sacred Laws of the Universe against which all other laws and rules may be measured. The first is the Law of Non-interference. Never do we have the right to interfere or choose for the lifestream of another, only for ourselves.

The second Law of the Universe is that we must be Non-judgmental. For it is in judging others that we set ourselves up to be judged. And by what measure are we capable of judging? For none of us are perfect. We live in an expression of creation which exists in a time-space continuum and where everything is, therefore, "measured". In that respect, common sense dictates that we must "measure" (or "judge") that which is around us. For example, we must judge whether or not a ladder is safe to climb or a school is good for our children, or a car is suitable to our needs. These daily "judgements" may be more properly termed "evaluations" and the expression of our responsibilities to ourselves and to others.

Being non-judgemental means that you may not like the actions of others around you as they express their will and it at variance to yours, but you do not judge them to be "wrong" and yourself to be "right". Become conscious of when you are passing judgement on others and try to avoid the temptation, but do not fret over it. As you progress along the pathways of detachemt and unconditional love you will find yourself automatically less and less inclined to make judgements of others.

"God gave you the kindling, you must light the fire."

Nineteen

Q: What is the highest expression of love for human beings?

G: Human love? Perhaps the greatest expression of *human* love is that you lay down your life for your brother. That you yourself would be willing, for example, to give your life for the sake of your child or your husband. In that act of self-sacrifice, you are expressing the selflessness of divine love through the human form. Having once been touched by *divine* love, you will surely reach a point where you are truly set upon experiencing unity with the Creator, and then you will have no attachment to anything on this planet. So every aspect of your life is for love of your brother. By choice you will give up everything that will constitute your control of your life. You will willingly sacrifice your specialized, ego-driven, self-propelled, self-willed expression of your life on this planet. You would be as if you had never been. You would give yourself no value in name, or importance in works or deeds. You would lay all the potential for the experience of living this life before the feet of the Creator and say, *"I offer it all to you. How do you wish me to use the energy of my life? If you want me to die right this minute, I'll die. If you want me to go into a convent, I'll go into a convent. If you want me to scrub floors, I'll scrub floors."* Your life having been laid at the feet of the Creator, becomes driven by the Creator, and whatever use you make of your life after is the Creator's use.

The only problem with this is that if you are one who would like to become "religious", whether it be Buddhist, Christian, Hindu, etc., you are going to be confined within the Orders of that religion. And you are going to have a *physical* "spiritual director" who is going to discipline you one way or another according to *their* best understanding of what you need to fulfill the commitment you have made of sacrifice to the Creator for His love. But when you are living out in the world, you have no such discipline or direction, except that which you impose upon yourself, and that which comes from within.

I think that this is, perhaps, the challenge of this century and the challenge of the "age" we are moving into. That we can be self-disciplined beings who are saying, *"There is nothing of this life that I want as an expression of my ego. I wholly want the energy of this life to be used for the love and glory of the Creator. And I am seeking, in the best way I can, the inner directions so that I can fulfill my commitment to the Creator. And in so doing avoid the "illusion" which comes out of my knowledge and understanding."* Connection with the Divine Mind is something which is beyond knowledge and beyond understanding. The Creator is truly a mystery. Once you have been touched by that *mystery*, you will never forget. That experience is something that you will willingly devote the rest of your life to seeking in an effort to make it your permanent reality in this life experience.

The danger comes in that we don't just have an "attorney" in our heads, we have a whole "law firm" that justifies almost everything we want to do. And in that process, we can go within and pray and meditate and come back with all the answers about what we "should" be doing and delude ourselves into believing that this information is coming from Spirit. When in reality we are simply talking to ourselves in our heads. This happens very often with people. How often do you enter your quiet time with prayerful intent to "listen" to God, and instead, find yourself having a long one-sided discussion with yourself? It happens to all of us, especially when we have things on our mind which we think God would be particularly interested in! If I may suggest, try a simple prayer with as few words as possible. An often repeated, *"Help!"* will serve. You see God knows what is in our hearts and our minds and really doesn't need a lot of explanation, however beautifully worded.

TWENTY

Q: HOW DOES ONE AVOID CONTINUAL DELUSION?

G: There is a parallel road to the perfection of your soul. One of the parallel roads is humility. The other is unconditional love. You avoid delusion by learning to love unconditionally. Learning to love as Christ loved, equally and with humility. Without humility, you are not going to be able to avoid self-delusion. You will find yourself unable to avoid delusion so long as you have one shred of the personality ego which is still attached to the material illusion and therefore, capable of deluding you. It is the difficulty that I was referring to earlier in regard to detachment. When you have a "spiritual director" in the physical world, they will ensure that you keep the "rules". When you are out in the world, trying to walk the path to fulfill the concept which says, *"Be in the world, but not of the world"*, when you are truly trying to work towards "Christ Consciousness" in this way, the way to do it is to examine everything from the aspects of unconditional love and humility. If any situation in life causes you humiliation, whatever it is, then you are not being humble, because if you were humble, you would be without ego. And if you had no ego, how could you feel humiliation?

If you run a check with yourself of all your actions and reactions, and ask, *"Does this make me uncomfortable? Do I find it humiliating to go and beg for something?"* For example, I have no winter shoes and it is snowing. Does it embarrass me or make me feel uncomfortable to go to someone who has a great deal and ask, *"Could you possibly give me a pair of old shoes that are waterproof?"* Would I feel humiliated by having to do that? If you feel humiliated by asking for help, then you are not yet humble because the humble person expects nothing and is grateful for whatever comes to them.

That brings us to expectation. In having an expectation of someone, we are preempting their right to chose, thereby breaking the first Law of the Universe. And we are also making a judgment that they can and should fulfill our expectation, thereby, breaking the second Law of the Universe. Expectations can really lead to our downfall because it is out of our expectations that we suffer hurt and humiliation. When another person fails to live up to our expectations, we feel hurt by it, but point in fact, we are only hurting ourselves. Sometimes it is good for us to be hurt and humiliated as it can have a true humbling effect on the ego.

On the other hand when we love unconditionally and without expectation or anticipation of any action, return or reward from the object of our unconditional love, then no matter what they choose, we will not be personally hurt of offended by it.

TWENTY-ONE

Q: HOW WOULD ONE KNOW IF ONE WAS EXPRESSING UNCONDITIONAL LOVE?

G: The first expression of unconditional love is *"minding your own business."*

If you see a problem, it is a matter of discernment. The discernment comes as humility grows within you and you become a humble person. Then you can see clearly what needs to be done. As a humble person who is working through the expression of unconditional love or Divine Love, you are seeing with eyes of the Divine Mind. When you see with those eyes, you see a situation which needs help and you give that help in accordance with the divine promptings of your connection with Divine Mind.

When you have not yet reached that level, you may see a situation and your own ego tells you that situation needs help. And then you rush in there and say, *"I am a very loving person and I am humble enough to come to your poor home and get all of the dirt out of it and the fleas and the bugs and clean your house. And I will help you do all this so you can live as a clean and decent person."* You may feel that you are doing something wonderful for this poor person who lives in shocking circumstances, in a tar paper hut, which is filthy dirty because they have no means of doing anything with it, and you may feel you are doing a wonderful "good deed" there. Certainly the person is going to going to benefit by getting rid of the bugs and fleas, but your soul is not going to benefit because you went there, not out of unconditional love, but out of the conditional perception of your ego.

"The practice of detachment is one of selective attachment."

Twenty-Two

Q: WHEN ONE WHO CALLS YOU "FRIEND" COMES TO YOU FOR ADVISE OR SUPPORT, HOW WOULD YOU RESPOND TO THEM IN A WAY THAT WAS, "MINDING YOUR OWN BUSINESS"?

G: Respond to their need as they ask for it. For example, if a friend of yours comes along and complains of all her cuts and bruises because her husband beat her and says to you, *"Will you please help me?"* Attend to her cuts and bruises. Offer her a safe place to stay and suggest that she get whatever help is available. Give her the phone number of the Battered Wive's Home, or the health clinic. That is giving her the help she is asking for.

To then pursue it by saying, *"Now I advise you to leave him. I think you should pack your bags and move out,"* is unwarranted. It might be good advise from her point of view, but it is unwarranted because it is not what she has asked for. Give the help that is asked for to whomever asks. And give the help that *they* want, not the help that *you* think they should have.

If they ask you what you would do in the same situation, you are warranted in telling them what you would do *as it relates to you*, in that the actions *you* would take in similar circumstances may be totally inappropriate for them. The last thing you would want to do would be to influence their choice and thereby create for yourself an emotional tie to this planet. Be very careful with this. Ask yourself first is the opinion that you are expressing coming out of Divine Inspiration, or is it coming out of your knowledge and experience living on this planet? If it is coming out of knowledge and experience from living on this planet, then by giving it you are creating new emotional ties and karmic responsibilities. You are influencing another lifestream on the planet and by doing so you will accrue karmic responsibility for the outcome.

To define this more clearly, I think one of the things Christ said which is relevant is, *"Render unto Caesar that which is Caesar's and unto God that which is God's."* And here we are trying to address the question, *"How can one live in this world, but not be of this world?"* This is a clear example of how you can do this. You can live in this world and still render unto God that which is God's and unto Caesar that which is Caesar's. For example, the aspect of giving advise is, if you like, Caesar's coin, and it is best you don't have anything to do with it. Give the help that is asked for and don't be tempted to express your opinions.

When you express your opinion you are involving in their life, through that opinion. So how can you be doing that and walking and moving toward the path of detachment and connection only with Divine Mind? When your opinions, and the need to express them, are coming from your ego you are no longer focused on "God", but instead on "Caesar".

So if someone asks you what they might do to solve a problem they have, you might say, *"What have you thought of to do about this?"* And then simply listen to them. It would be a kindness to them to listen and to hear what they have thought about. You may listen to the choices they have thought of and offer them another way to see the problem and solutions. There is nothing wrong with that. Just keep this thought in mind; one military man once said, *"Define your mission."* So are you defining your mission as someone who wants to be wholly involved in this world and solving other people's problems for them, or are you defining your mission as the perfection of your own soul? If you are focused on the perfection of your own soul and union with the Divine Mind, then you don't want to be involving in other people's lives. And I use the word "involving", not "helping" in other people's problems. As soon as you start giving advice on ways to go, how to think and how to look at the problem, you are involving in that person's problems.

Now, once you have accomplished perfection of your own soul and are united with Divine Mind, then you are truly able to assist them with their problems. Again we have the perfect teaching by Christ for this: *"Why do you worry about the splinter in your brother's eye when you don't see the log in your own?"* — Matthew 7:13.

Remember any opinions or advice you give are only coming from your own perspective and so you have to ask yourself: Is my understanding and perspective perfect? Is it coming from Divine Mind? Most probably not. The example in history of this is with Marie Antoinette. When it was reported to her that the French were rioting and revolting and screaming for bread because they were starving, her response was, *"Let them eat cake."* From her perspective telling them to eat cake when they had no bread was a perfectly reasonable and logical thing to say, but it had absolutely no relationship to what was being asked for. This reaffirms what I said earlier that in order for our opinions to begin to have value, they must first be objective, not subjective.

So in order for us to walk the path objectively toward the perfection of our souls, so that we do not find ourselves developing more karmic ties and emotional attachments, then what we must be ever cognizant of is being able to discern the difference between offering the help that is needed, or asked for, and letting go of the urge, whether it is requested or not, to offer our opinions.

It really is much simpler than it sounds, to govern ourselves objectively, if we just remember the two rules I spoke of earlier: *The first rule of the Universe is Non-Interference with the lifestream of another.* (Your opinion, if followed, may cause someone to change the flow of their life). *The second rule of the Universe is be Non-Judgemental.* (Whenever you express opinions, you are making judgments.)

We do not have to be frightened of involving with others just to protect our own ego from the consequences caused by a lack of discernment on our part. If we check our motives and actions against those two universal rules, we will not easily fall into error and, with a little self-discipline and practice, we will soon find ourselves re-opening our connection with the Source, and therefore, be able to be of "beneficial" help to those in need who call upon us.

How many of us can remember in our early childhood having some favorite aunt who we absolutely adored and who truly loved us? She really simply loved us. She never made us eat the things we did not like, or demanded that we clean our plate. She never cared whether or not we washed our face. She never cared if we tore our clothes and got dirty when we went on picnics. She just loved us and enjoyed seeing us having a wonderful time. It wasn't that we misbehaved. It wasn't that she was without discipline, but that the whole energy of being with that favorite aunt was that we just knew we were loved and we'd have a wonderful time with her.

That aunt was very much involving in our lives, but she was not being judgmental. She wasn't expressing an opinion. She wasn't saying *"you should clean your plate"*. "You *should* keep your clothes clean"'. *"You shouldn't play those dangerous games."* Life was not full of *shoulds* and *should nots* with her. You can become the "favorite" aunt to humanity and people will flock around you, but you won't be telling them what to do.

It is wonderful to be there for people when they ask you to be there for them, just don't tell them what to do. As soon as you start telling someone what to do, you are taking away their choice and their choices are their growing opportunities. That is how we learn and how we evolve ourselves, by learning to discern and make our own choices.

Twenty-Three

Q: IF YOU ARE NOT INVOLVED WITH HUMANITY OR PEOPLE IN A WAY THAT IS CAUSING ATTACHMENT, THEN WHAT IS YOUR LIFE EXPRESSING?

G: You are involved in life, in the whole process. You are involved in evolution in life as a whole. To date it sounds as if what we're saying is very selfish, very self-oriented, but it isn't. There was an experiment done some years ago where some rats were taught to go through a particular maze to get food. It was discovered that a short time later, all the rats in Australia knew how to go through that maze, even though that experiment was done in the United States. Because of the mass consciousness of the rats, the information permeated out into the consciousness and became part of the memory of all rats, and that is true of all living things.

For example, if you in your entire lifetime did nothing, had no contact with any other person and were completely isolated, but in that isolation were focused on the perfection of your own soul and so achieved, by the complete sacrifice of your life, union with the Divine Mind, then that amount of energy created in you would permeate the whole consciousness of humanity. Every single person alive would benefit by what you had done.

There is a teaching here as well that relates to this. *"Never let your left hand know what your right hand is doing."* What you do that is unseen and unknown is almost always more important than what you do that everybody sees and hears. Humanity is one aspect of life. You are an aspect of life and you are expressing whatever you choose to express and in whatever way you choose to express it. Unconditional love is not something you *feel*. It is something *you are*. And when you become unconditional love, that is what your life will be expressing.

TWENTY-FOUR

Q: EXPLAIN WHAT YOU MEAN BY THE TERM "EGO" AND HOW THE HUMAN EGO WAS DEVELOPED? ALSO IS THERE AN EGO BEYOND THE HUMAN EGO?

G: When we speak of the ego we are usually referring to the ego of the personality. When we came to this planet in this lifetime we each brought with us a part of our soul which had a plan for all the lessons it needed to learn in this life. During our birth into the physical world most of us passed through the "veil of forgetfulness" and our souls lay quiet in our breast while we each developed the ego of this body. Our ego evolves from our culture, environment, education, genetic history—all the things which we experience which make up the "I" we each are most familiar with. Therefore, the personality ego might be said to be our *opinion* of ourselves as opposed to our *awareness* of ourselves.

As time passes our personality ego becomes stronger and stronger. It sets goals to achieve its wants; material success and the accompanying material possessions, academic achievement, power, piety, sainthood, whatever the personality perceives as "fulfillment". And it is this ego of the personality which exercises our free will in life.

Yet in all of this "striving for material goals", what has happened to the needs of the soul? They tend to be "forgotten". It is now the time of "remembering" who you are, and to do this you must begin to listen to your soul; that part of you which connects you to the Creator, and through which, the needs of your soul can be fulfilled.

With that in mind remember that our ego is a very necessary part of our being. For it is the ego which sustains us as individual thinking beings during the period when we are growing and maturing to that point when we become truly aware of ourselves as immortal beings having the potential for an immortal soul. Once we become aware of our potential as immortal beings, we then need to shed the ego of the personality in order to allow the flowering of the true ego of ourselves; the ego of our immortal being.

TWENTY-FIVE

Q: PLEASE SHARE WHAT YOU KNOW ABOUT THE UNIVERSE.

G: Webster's dictionary tells us that the word comes from the Latin "universum", meaning "all together". The universe comprises all that IS. That which is made manifest and brought into existence is the direct effect of a cause, the reaction to an action. My understanding is that the Action of Creation is the emission of *sound*. Think of it this way; when a singer holds a certain tone a glass can be shattered. The *sound* vibrations are collectively responsible for this. Now imagine reversing the process and putting the glass back together. Do you get the idea?

In the Book of Genesis it does not tell us that God formed light or made light, it says, "And God SAID let there be light". In other words, a *sound* issued forth from the Source and the reaction to that action was the appearance of light. When you extend this idea you can see how important the *naming* of anything is, for as you *name* you create.

Modern psychology is expressing an understanding of this principle when it tells you that if you call a child "bad" often enough, they will be "bad" and if you praise them, they will develop "good" traits. Talking to plants, playing Mozart to cows in the barn, singing a child to sleep, creating a universe; these are all utilizing the principle of *sound*. So, mirror the Creator and let the sounds which come from you create "good" and harmonious things for yourself and others.

"A child is both the future and the past."

TWENTY-SIX

Q: HOW MANY CYCLES ARE THERE IN THIS CREATION?

G: Once the Creation was made manifest its evolutionary movement took the form of a convoluted curve. This spiral is infinite. And, as I said earlier, the lesser cycles on the spiral complete themselves approximately every 50,000 years. For a clearer understanding of this process see the drawings on the following pages 64 and 65.

BECOMING = BEING

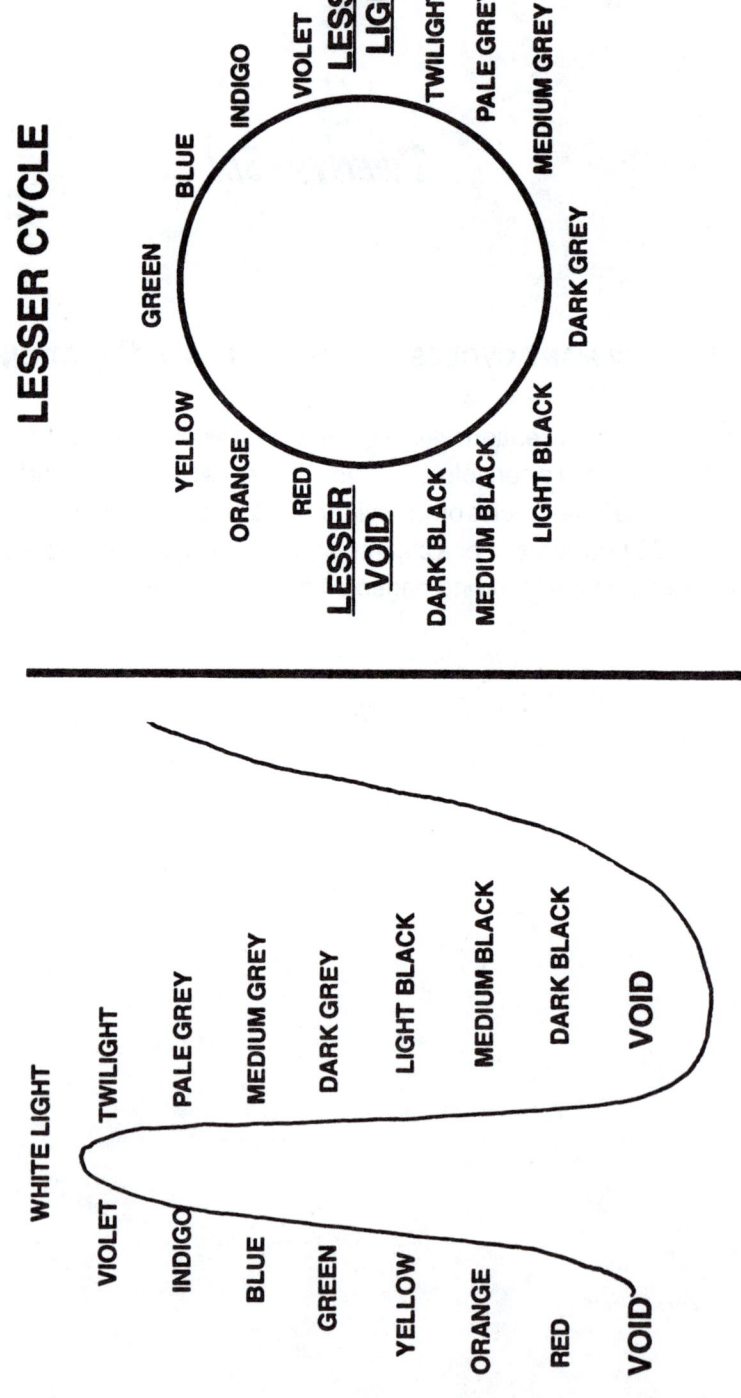

LESSER CYCLE

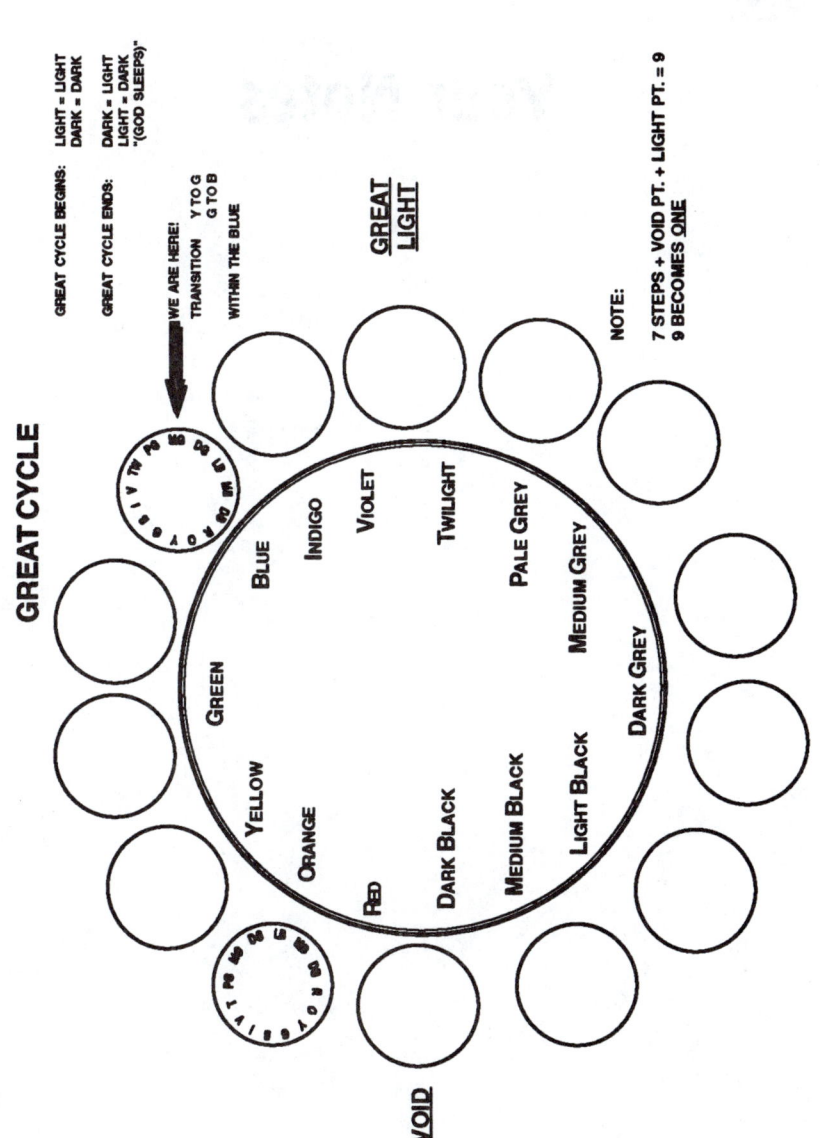

Your Notes

TWENTY-SEVEN

Q: MUST WE ACHIEVE CHRIST CONSCIOUSNESS DURING THIS LIFETIME, BY THE END OF THIS CYCLE, IN ORDER TO RETAIN OUR IMMORTALITY AND MOVE ON?

G: Whether we have achieved Christ Consciousness or not, is a judgment made by the Highest Authority and not by ourselves. What we must achieve within ourselves is the total *absolute* commitment to the path of Christ Consciousness and the *absolute* abandonment to the love and mercy of God. That is what will qualify us to evolve to the next level of experience. If one has not totally completed that lesson of Christ Consciousness, then I am sure you will be afforded the opportunity elsewhere. It is the *commitment* to the path which is required, in objective honesty, because there really is no way you can know of yourself, that you achieved or have not achieved.

It may be that one good deed in our life will qualify us. It may be that it requires a whole lifetime to qualify us. That is not for us to judge. What I am certain of is that unless we have made the internal commitment and are doing our best to fulfill that commitment, we don't stand a chance of igniting that flame within ourselves. That is the requirement for our continued evolution.

In addition, it may be that Christ Consciousness is only that level of perfection which moves us from this cycle of reincarnations into the next cycle. Or it may be that Christ Consciousness is the ultimate level of perfection that we need. That I don't know. I have no idea what the final exam is that God sets for us. But I do know that we must walk the path and must walk it with wholehearted commitment. Christ said, *"No man, having put his hand to the plough, and looking back, is fit for the Kingdom of God."* — Luke 9:62. I have always understood that to mean that once you say you are working towards your spiritual evolution, once you say you have made that commitment, you better stick with it. You had better not try to change your mind. Because it is better to have no pretense of commitment to God, than to have made a commitment to God which falls short of the demands made upon it.

TWENTY -EIGHT

Q: IS BALANCING THE CHAKRA LEVELS IN YOUR BODY EQUAL TO CHRIST CONSCIOUSNESS?

G: Let me explain it this way. There are meditative techniques which allow you to activate and manipulate your energy field in such a way that you activate the chakras one by one. So you can sit and do a specific meditation which takes you through chakras one through twelve and you can focus your intent and tell these chakras to operate and move — they will do so and come into balance. And for that moment you will be emitting the white light. That is true and that white light emission is a manifestation of Christ Consciousness within you. It is a point of perfect balance.

Let us say that you do that one morning and achieve it and you hold it for ten, twenty, thirty seconds and then you come out of your meditative state and you go out into the world and start telling other people what to do; ordering people about, being unpleasant and generally not behaving too well. How long do you think you are going to maintain that balance? If the only state that you can maintain it in is when you are focused and meditating, then it is an artificially created state. It is not the natural instinctive state for you.

So, where it is of great benefit to bring the chakras into balance, it certainly isn't the whole story. Every area of your life has to be in balance. Remember Christ says, *"By their works they will be known."* So you not only have to have the intent, you have to be living the intent.

"The road to hell is paved with good intentions." That is one of my favorite statements because it reminds me constantly of how quickly we fall short. Conversely, if you are someone who has never heard of chakras, but you are living in perfect balance and harmony on all four planes of your existence, you can be certain that if some clairvoyant looks at your energy field and your chakras, they will see every single one of them is perfect and in balance.

The exception would be in any lifetime when someone is declaring themselves to be an Atheist. The progression of their soul in that lifetime is not possible, because their denial of the Creator is intrinsically tied to their own lack of humility. And as we said before, the two prerequisites for the evolution of your soul are unconditional love and humility. Without those, your soul cannot and will not progress no matter how much time is devoted to the energy fields we call "chakras". Beyond that particular life, however, the professed Atheist will be able to look back and see the effect of his beliefs and learn from the experience for his "future".

TWENTY-NINE

Q: WHAT ABOUT AGNOSTICS?

G: Agnostics are simply people who are questioning. That is something which we should all do. Unfortunately, too many people accept a packaged belief structure handed down to them by someone else. Accepting a packaged belief structure is exactly the same as putting blinders on a horse. You preclude all other possibilities. You narrow your field of vision and in that process you are not progressing your soul, because you are not allowing for the expansion of your awareness through your own insights. You are not investigating and progressing your own truth. It is our own truth upon which we should stand, not someone else's. We cannot by the very nature of energy, alter our own spiritual state by accepting someone else's truth.

There are many pathways back to God, but there is only *one* way to walk any of those paths and that is with objective truth and honesty. Objective truth in your own soul. That is to say that it has to be your truth, and it has to be a truth which is clear to you beyond your ego, beyond your opinion. If a particular religion is chosen because it is a form of worship which you find aids you in your personal progress back to the Creator— in your personal quest for union with the Creator—directly between your soul and the Creator, then the form of that religion may serve you well. But if you view the religion to which you adhere from the point of view of, *"This person says this is what I must believe, and if I believe him then I don't have to worry about my soul,"* then you are going to find that you're sadly mistaken and you have a lot of ground to make up at a later time.

It is true that Christ promised eternal life to believers. I think here as with all teachings in the Bible, we have to keep in mind that [the Bible] has been translated many times. However my guidance tells me that most of the words spoken by Christ are accurately translated in the New Testament. Bearing that in mind, we can look at exactly what Christ said, and I paraphrase, *"He who believes in me, believes in my teachings, believes in what I am telling them, will find a way to salvation."* He did not say, *"He who believes in the structure of the church set up by XYZ and in their interpretation of what I am saying, and in the rules and laws which they set down for their church, they will be saved."* If someone chooses to adhere to those rules and laws set down by a church doctrine, that is their free choice. But let them not make the mistake in thinking that because they don't eat fish on Friday or they go to a particular service on a Saturday, or they only speak to people of the same faith, or they only go into the churches of the same faith, or they don't marry anyone of a different faith, that by following these rules they will save their souls, because they will not. Those are not the teachings that Christ gave at all. Those are the teachings that man has devolved. And it is because of those teachings which man has *de*volved throughout the centuries, that we are basically in so much trouble today.

THIRTY

Q: WHAT WOULD YOU SAY TO SOMEONE WHO PROFESSES THE NEED OR DESIRE TO "HELP" PEOPLE OR HUMANITY, CALLING IT A NEED TO SERVE?

G: First I would say to them, *"Physician heal thyself."* Before you start going out and healing humanity, or raising the consciousness of every person you meet, raise your own consciousness, heal your own ills. Of course we are speaking in generalities here because there are always exceptions to the rule, but very often those who are out there being of service as they perceive service, are people whose own lives are unsatisfactory and they are so unhappy with themselves, that the only way they can stay alive is by focusing all there energy into something for someone else.

The ideal person to be of service is one who has achieved for himself and is now able to give of that achievement to others. That is true in all areas of life. Both on the material plane and in the spiritual plane, that is true. For instance, would you really want a financial planner who had gone bankrupt? Wouldn't it be nice if someone had made millions of dollars and decided they did not need to make any more for themselves, so they would now be a financial planner and help other people. I think you'd feel far more comfortable trusting your resources to that person than to the bankrupt person. Sadly, there are many people out there who are involved in the spiritual well-being of others who are spiritually bankrupt themselves. We can't take gold out of an empty purse and we can't take Divine Wisdom out of a heart which does not live by unconditional love.

This is another example of hypocrisy. But if you were to say to these people, *"You are acting hypocritically,"* they would be devastated because their efforts, very often, come out of sincere beliefs. The catch is that they are attached to beliefs that have no real meaning or validity. They are attached to other peoples truths, to things that they have been told, not to their own connection to the Creator. There are vast millions on this planet who are told and believe, through their religious instruction, that the only way that they can connect with the Creator is through some minister, or priest or dogma that is laid down for them and sets rules to abide by. That is not true. The connection to the Creator is within the individual heart. It is a very real place at the base of the heart where the material and spiritual connection is made. This is the *Chalice of the Soul* where lives the immortal essence, only awaiting you to join heart and mind and so kindle the eternal Three-Fold Flame. You can take the dogma and the rules as taught to you and you can put them into practice, but unless you *know* those things to be true within your own heart, they will serve you nothing.

THIRTY-ONE

Q: WHY DO YOU USE THE MASCULINE TERMINOLOGY WHEN REFERRING TO GOD?

G: All energy is neutral. God is neither male nor female, God simply is. The reason I choose to use the masculine as identification is because if you ever have the experience of literally *"hearing the voice of God,"* you will realize the tonal frequency on which that identity personified communicates, is an extremely low vibratory frequecy—a frequency so low that no average female voice could possibly register it.

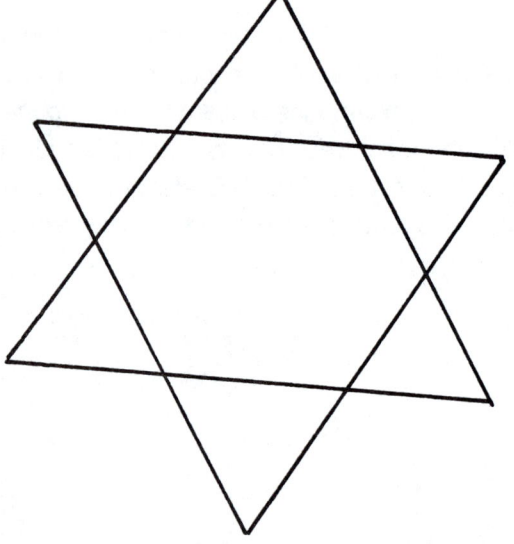

Thirty-Two

Q: Does one's particular work for God come to him/ her as insight?

G: It comes through prayer, insight and meditation. Through these means, you will come to an inner knowing of what you should do. Examine your own soul and determine in whatever ways are available to you what your soul needs to do in a lifetime to assist its growth towards its perfection. What do you do with your physical being to fulfill your soul's purpose? Do you go out and nurse the lepers, work for the poor, devote yourself to the homeless and then turn around and say, *"I am being of service to humanity and the planet and, therefore, I am evolving my soul."* That is not necessarily true. You may not be evolving your soul at all. The very fact that you feel you are evolving and that your service is going to automatically promote your soul's growth negates most of the growth you are going to get from the service.

It is true that the lepers, the poor and the homeless are going to be helped by your work with them. They are going to benefit from your efforts, but it is possible that you will not. Because we must be ever aware of our tendencies toward *hypocrisy*, our keen and objective discernment is of utmost importance when we assess our intent and the spiritual value of all which we chose to do.

Hypocrisy often grows out of our desire to think well of ourselves and to have others think well of us. It can be a huge block to any soul's growth. Christ said he came to the planet to save "sinners", and the healthy don't need a doctor. It always seems to me that God is nearer to an honest sinner than to a hypocritical "good" man. Spirit does not measure as a human does. If we try to obtain the *objective*, rather than the subjective view of ourselves, we will find it becomes more and more difficult to be hypocritical. We involve in hypocrisy to maintain the illusions of our ego. As we shed the ego of the personality so we remove ourselves from hypocritical action.

Thirty-Three

Q: Presuming that we desire to maintain spiritual balance in our interrelationships, how would we respond to negative, blameful and angry emotional energy that another is thrusting toward us?

G: Love your enemies, turn the other cheek. So if you are then able to actually turn the other cheek, and let it go, the question you must ask yourself is, are you turning the other cheek and thinking, *"What a good Christian I am because I am following the precepts of Christ and turning the other cheek."* Beware of false piety. Could we be turning the other cheek to avoid giving emotional pain? If you believe that your intention is that you are trying to avoid causing them more *emotional* pain then I have to go back to when I spoke of objective honesty. You have to walk your own truth. Nobody at any point in time knows all the truth. Nobody. So first you have to find what is your truth and then you have to have the courage to live it.

Do you think Christ would have taken action to cause pain? Well he did, didn't he? Remember the incident in the temple, when he threw out all the moneychangers? When he overthrew the moneychangers in the temple, that must have caused them great pain and suffering to see all their ill-gotten gains going by the wayside. So in answer to the question of *"Do you avoid something because you don't want to give pain,"* that depends on whether that is your truth or not. If you are concerned about giving or receiving *emotional* pain at the material level, then are you being humble? If you are truly a humble person, it will not occur to you that you could give pain, simply because you will always see the other person as bigger, stronger and better than you are, *spiritually speaking*, and you will instead, question your own actions to see how you may have been at fault and how you may have provoked the other person. We look first to ourselves, because we realize that we are never justified for casting all blame away from ourselves for the discordant circumstances we may find ourselves in.

It is this twin staff of love and humility. If you have love and humility you will not take "wrong" actions at any level of your life. But without humility and without love no matter what rules you live by, no matter what dogma you follow, no matter what religious beliefs you adhere to, you will not achieve perfection of your soul and Divine Union. Of course this opens up a whole can of worms because almost every religion says that theirs is the only "true" and "right" religion. There is no humility in saying you're the only one who is "right". Absolutely none.

If someone says, *"I have looked at my spirituality, I have looked at how I can grow spiritually and I believe that, by following the precepts of this particular religion or form of teaching, I can help myself grow and this feels right to me".* I say, *"Wonderful! Join that religion, adhere to its teachings and make your progress in that way because there are many, many pathways back to God. Just remember the way to walk that path is with absolute **objective honesty**."* So if you have made the statement that you choose to adhere to the teachings of a particular religion because it feels right to you, that is wonderful. But if you are walking that path with objective honesty, you will be honest enough to say that it may not be the path for everyone. Therefore, you will not claim your path as the only path, neither will you condemn the pathways that other people choose to walk. It has been said that all roads lead to Rome. I say, *all spiritual paths* lead to God.

Thirty-Four

Q: PLEASE EXPLAIN WHAT INTUITION IS AND HOW IT WORKS.

G: In general, first impressions or intuitions are our best guidance when we are on this planet. Sadly, we tend not to follow them. We, instead, receive an intuition and then we "think" about it—and "thinking" gets in the way of our intelligence. Our intelligence is an intuitive intelligence that naturally flows in harmony with all of creation. It makes us aware of all things at all times and we can intuit what the response to something would be. So then that intuitive response will invariably be far more accurate than if we start analyzing it, thinking about it and reorganizing it.

An intuitive response is just a response. It has no judgment in it. It is rather like running along a cliff and you come to the edge of the precipice and your intuition says, *"Stop!,"* so you stop. There is no judgment. Judgment then comes in when you start to think about *why* you stopped. Then judgement is going to say to you that this was a wise decision to stop because, otherwise, you would have gone over the cliff. So intuition comes in before judgment gets into the picture. If you run your life on intuition, you are not making judgments.

Interestingly enough your intuitive responses are tied to your level of evolution. Your spiritual growth is never lost from lifetime to lifetime. It carries from one lifestream to another. Whatever level of spiritual awareness you reach in one lifetime is the base level of your spirituality in the next one. You may go forward or backwards along that line during the lifetime, but from whatever level of development you leave the lifetime, you will begin the next lifetime with that level of spiritual development. That level of spiritual development is your intuition. It is what comes through to you as intuitive response and it comes out of the chakra levels. For example, if you are operating out of a gross survival level at the most animalistic stage of development, then your intuitive response, if you saw something you wanted which someone else possessed, would be to hit them over the head with a rock and take it from them. That would be your intuitive response, because you are operating out of the base survival instincts, out of the unrefined root chakra.

If you have increased you vibratory frequencies energetically with your spiritual growth so that you are now operating out of your unrefined solar plexus chakra, then your intuitive responses will be the ones that tell you how best to live in the material world. We live in the material world on that vibratory frequency of the emotional body expressing at the solar plexus chakra level. When you have mastered living on this planet as a physical human being, and you are living in harmony on this planet, then your instinctive responses are coming from the solar plexus. You developed in the third chakra level an instinctive response and that is where your level of intuition will come from.

When you have evolved beyond that level and you are moving up to the understanding of true compassion and unconditional love, you are expressing those qualities out of your throat chakra, which is where you express unconditional love. If your vibratory frequency is at the throat chakra level, then every intuition you express is going to be one fueled by unconditional love. So your intuition is the clear expression of the level of spiritual growth which you have achieved at this point.

Now regarding premonitions or visions. As we have the exercise of free-will as a God-given gift, I view all premonitions, visions and clairvoyant insights to be information designed to forewarn us so we can change our future. So we can, if we so choose, alter the outcome of the situations which are in front of us, insofar as they are our responsibility and are properly within the realm of our right to choose.

Thirty-Five

Q: WHERE DOES "DISCERNMENT" END AND "JUDGEMENT" BEGIN?

G: The way you begin to sort out whether you are making a discerning choice or passing a judgement is to ask *"Why?"* For example, *"Why don't I want to involve with that person in business?"* If you say in response, *"It is because I personally don't like that individual and my knowledge of that person is that they are dishonest. And also it is not a business I want to be in and I do not believe the business will be successful,"* then that's a reasonable evaluation of the question and a reasonably discerning choice. But if you are saying, *"I don't want to involve myself with that person in business because they don't attend church and I think they should,"* then you are making a judgement. There is nothing wrong with judgement as long as it is appropriate. Discernment is appropriate judgement or appropriate evaluation.

Being judgmental is condemning someone or some situation without all the knowledge of that situation. You are making a judgement without having all of the information. And nobody ever has all the information about someone else, because someone else is an accumulation of many past lives, many experiences that are not known at any one point in time. So you can never be judgmental, not even of yourself, unless you are aware of all your lives and experiences from your beginning. Even then you can only be discerning. That discernment requires you to make appropriate judgement in the light of the knowledge you have at that given time, particularly when it relates to how you live. This is called Personal Responsibility. The exception to the rule is in regard to parential responsibility. Parents have a responsibility with young children to make certain judgements; let's say for arguments sake, that it is probably not good for the child to sit in front of the TV for ten hours a day. That is a solid judgement. That is not the parent being judgmental. The parents are *being* judgmental if they say, *"All television is bad, therefore, you can't watch television."* To say to the child, *"You are only allowed two hours of television a day because more is not good for you,"* is making a discerning judgement in light of the knowledge you have about television.

Thirty-Six

Q: How would you describe empathy and mercy?

G: Empathy, on the human level, is the ability of the *personality* to directly relate to someone else's situation or feelings. Personality is the outward expression of the ego. If one has shed the ego of the personality and evolved the *true self* of the soul, then empathy at the *soul* level can occur. In this way, empathy may be related to unconditional love and compassion, and compassion has no *human* emotion in it.

For example, if you find yourself feeling the "pain" of another individual's personal circumstance, as though *you* have experienced it personally, then your response would be empathetic, *provided* you were feeling their pain and not feeling emotional because of it. Even sadness is an emotion. Spiritual empathy has no emotion. It is related to compassion. If I can feel your pain, I have no attachment to it. It is not my pain—it is your pain. But I can feel it because I am empathic.

Whether or not I can *understand* your pain is irrelevant. Empathy is the ability to directly connect with somebody else's experience. If you are attached to it. If it makes you feel happy. If it makes you feel sad. If it makes you want to do something for them. If it makes you want to stay away from them. Those are emotions and are to do with the empathetic nature of your personality.

You can have empathy and feel emotion. In fact, most people do and then they run about saying, *"I am so empathetic with people and that's how I can help them."* This is a lack of understanding about empathy because the very emotion which they feel shows the empathy is based in their personality, and therefore, the help they give is coming from ego. Or, on the other hand, someone says, "I am so empathetic that I have to stay away from people." That is nonsense. They are being affected and so are attached to an emotion. This is not an expression of compassion. This person has, somewhere within themselves, developed enough unconditional love and compassion to be empathetic. But since they are affected emotionally by that event and are attached to it, they, therefore, are not fully able to express unconditional love and compassion.

Empathy does not necessarily require any action. Whether or not you take action is a matter of discernment and the exercise of your free will. For example, let's say you see a deer on the highway which was just struck down by a truck. It is mortally wounded, but not yet dead. So you make the decision to shoot it and put it out of its pain. To feel the pain that the deer is suffering is empathy. To decide to kill it to put it out of its pain is an act of kindness and no doubt an empathetic person would perform that act of kindness.

Empathy of the soul flowers as one begins to develop true compassion and unconditional love. One of the first things we may find developing when we have begun to open the heart chakra is spiritual empathy. The awareness of other people, other beings and other creatures. It is not tied into action. Because spiritual empathy is a very critical point in someone's spiritual growth, there is a tendency to get emotional and want to rush out and *do* something. The emotion belongs to the physical world, not to the spiritual world.

A person may have evolved themselves and truly opened the door to their ability to express unconditional love and compassion. They could be on the threshold of that stairway which takes them to Divine Union, and right on this first step, they turn their back on Divine Union, and instead, become emotionally involved with all the circumstances that they feel empathetically connected with. What this emotional empathy is doing is causing them to turn their back on their own evolution. The biggest problem we have is that we get in our own way and we perceive good and evil from the human perception, which is not God's perception. Emotional empathy of the personality can lead us to make false judgments, especially of what is "good" and what is "evil".

About *mercy*, I think probably Shakespeare said it better than I can when he wrote, *"The quality of mercy is not strained, but droppeth as the gentle rain from heaven."* Mercy is most definitely a God-like quality that we can attribute to the Creator...an aspect of the Creator. And it is something which is inherent in the nature of all humans. We all have the capability of being merciful should we so chose. Mercy is the expression of compassion for no particular reason.

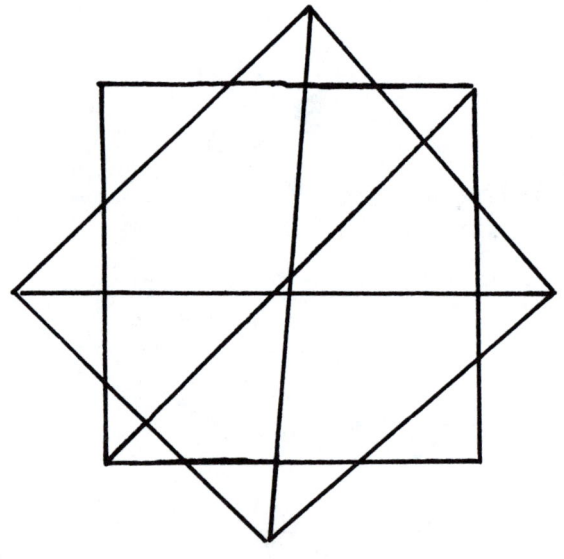

THIRTY-SEVEN

Q: WHAT IS THE TRUTH IN THE POPULAR STATEMENT, "WE CREATE OUR OWN REALITY?"

G: It is accurate to say that our own *perceptions* of reality define our reality. How we perceive things is how they are to us and that is our reality. In the broader sense, the experiences that we have make up our life in general. Our reactions are based upon our perception of those experiences and this defines our reality. The experience that we are living in is not necessarily something that we have created for ourselves, except in so far as we have allowed the experience.

I think the idea that is being promoted is that you "think" something and therefore you "create" something. That is true in the sense that energy follows thought, therefore what you think about is where the energy is placed and that energy will manifest itself. I feel where a lot of misconceptions come in is that someone who arrives at 35 years of age suddenly decides to become enlightened and start thinking for themselves and creating their reality, and twenty years later they wonder why they haven't yet created that reality — why it isn't the way they think it should be. It is because they had thirty-five previous years plus all the lifetimes before in which they were not consciously focusing their energy and their thinking on creating their reality. So what they have got, the experience they are living in, is an accumulation of not only everything they ever did, but everything which they allowed themselves to be affected by.

What I most often see is that people are concerning themselves with creating more wealth, prosperity, a mate, a bigger house, a better body, happiness—of all sorts of materially related things. And there is nothing wrong with having these things. What one must ask oneself is this; *if I am directing my energy to creating all of these things related to this world and my material comforts, am I doing God's will and fulfilling the perfection of my own soul?*

And the answer would be, *"Not very likely."* God does not care whether you are rich or poor, healthy or sick, intelligent or stupid. That is what *you* care about. *You* want to be beautiful and rich. *You* want to be smart and successful. That is all ego, and has absolutely nothing whatsoever to do with your relationship to your Creator.

You see, *"creating your own reality,"* means absolutely nothing, unless the reality you are creating is one of union with the Creator. But in order to do that, you are certainly not going to be focused on how to be rich and beautiful. You will have sacrificed everything. Yet it is absolutely true that the power of positive thinking can make you a millionaire, can make you successful, can make you rich. But if you want to evolve as a *spiritual* being, the only goal you can have, the only goal worth having is the perfection of your own soul. And the perfection of your own soul has nothing to do with being rich. You may be rich. There is nothing wrong with being rich, it is where you choose to place your focus. Where you choose to place your will and intent. If you are choosing to spend your days affirming that you will be rich, you will be successful and have all these things of the material world, then you are certainly being *of* the material world as well as *in* it.

To believe, espouse and try to live this *"we create our own reality"* mentality, then usually, you are setting yourself a trap if the reality you are trying to create is one of wealth, fame, beauty and success. It is because, through love of these things, you tie yourself emotionally to the material plane and consequently to the "round" of reincarnation.

One often hears the word "abundance". I'll program for myself *abundance*. The question you have to ask yourself is, *abundance of what?* If you want to create true abundance for yourself in the *spiritual* sense, then the only thing you would be wanting to create is an abundance of God's love within you, an abundance of compassion for your fellow humans, and an abundance of humility within yourself. If you have those three "abundances", then you have all you will ever need.

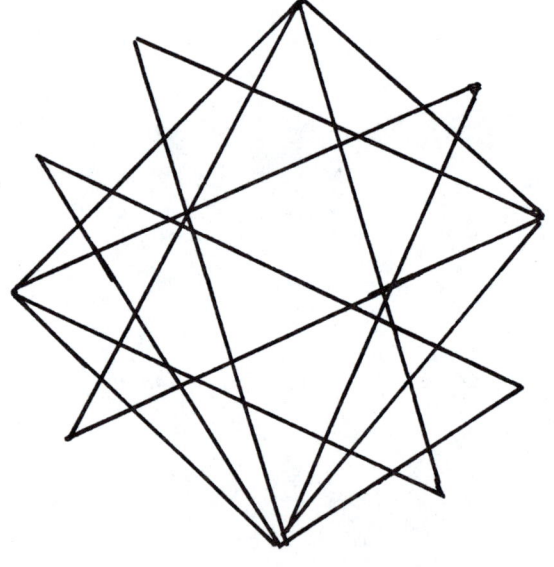

Thirty-Eight

Q: Speak about "illusion".

G. All that is is Life and Life is the One. All that exists is the illusion of the One. We are participants in the illusion we helped to create as part of the One. All the Hierarchies and dimensions, the concepts of spiritual evolution and progression, all are part of the illusion. When the circle of illusion is complete aeons from now, the illusion will cease to exist— *we* will cease to exist—and all will sink back into the timelessness of the One. This is Union with God.

Q: Wasn't Christ united with God and at the same time a participant in this illusion? In view of what you just said, how is that possible?

G: The One exists in timelessness and is, therefore, unaffected by the events of linear time. It is therefore possible to step out of timelessness and into time. Both time and timelessness exist concurrently and by their opposing nature, the one cannot intrude upon the other.

Q: Then how can the length of eternity as a measure of existence in time be determined?

G: Eternity as the measure of the duration of existence will be determined by the participants in the illusion of that existence by the amount of energy they are able to garner and return into the existence. Whenever an imbalance in the flow of energy being returned to the existence occurs, the existence itself is jeopardized. This is true for one man and for the whole cosmos.

Q: WHAT HAS THIS TO DO WITH CHRIST CONSCIOUSNESS?

G: Christ Consciousness is that state of perfect balance wherein the being is returning life energy to life and so supporting the existence.

Q: YOU SAID CHRIST WAS IN UNION WITH GOD AND STEPPED OUT OF TIMELESSNESS INTO TIME?

G: Exactly. It is the paradox of the illusion that the participants, man, are responsible for the maintaining of the existence in time, and yet, he is incapable of doing so unless he, himself, is also existing in timelessness.

Q: BUT I THOUGHT YOU SAID EXISTENCE IN TIMELESSNESS IS UNION WITH GOD AND IN THAT TOTAL UNION ALL TIME WOULD CEASE TO EXIST?

G: Yes. When the circle is complete, all are united with God in timelessness and the illusion existing in time will cease. When that occurs all is again the One from which the new Creation will spring.

THIRTY-NINE

Q.: WILL YOU OFFER AN EXPLANATION OF THE MEANING AND EXPRESSION OF FAITH AND GRACE?

G: Grace is that which is given by the Divine Creator through no effort of ours. Grace is a gift from God which we do not deserve. We have done absolutely nothing to earn or to deserve it — it is simply a gift.

Faith is an inner knowing, beyond reason and understanding, that the Creator exists, you are forever connected to the Creator, and you are forever a part of the creation.

Faith and grace. I would say in response, *"Except that you be as little children."* Thinking and reasoning are processes of evaluation. Does the small child of the loving parent ask itself the question, *"Does my mother love me?"* And then think and reason out the probable answer. No, the child knows, assumes and takes for granted, without thought or reasoning, that the mother loves it. That is Faith and we should accept God's love for us in the same unquestioning way. That faith and certainty of his love must be the rock and foundation upon which we build our lives. It may be that all of our life is falling apart around us, and no matter how hard we try we cannot, through our reason and understanding, make any sense of what is happening to us. But if we cling fast with that childlike certainty of God's love for us—if we keep faith—we can be sure that a way will open, understanding will come.

That understanding or enlightenment is *Grace*. A precious jewel given directly to the soul by the hand of God. It is not something we earn or deserve, but is the loving act of kindness of a parent to a child.

Many people say, *"I have faith that the Creator will provide for all my needs."* That is true. The Creator does provide for all our needs. The mistake one usually finds is that when people make that reference, they are often not referring to their needs. They are most often referring to their *wants*.

Many people also believe that if they are living in accordance with God's will that their lives here on Earth will be perfect. This is not true. Life on this planet is not perfect. Our emotional, mental and spiritual balance may perfect itself through the exercise of doing God's work— whatever God's work is for us— and in this way we may be able to maintain a perception that our physical reality is perfect for us despite any difficulty or hardship we may be enduring.

FORTY

Q: HOW DOES FAITH RELATE TO FAITH HEALING?

G: Let me tell you a story. You will remember how Christ was walking through a crowd of people and someone came up behind him and touched the hem of his garment. He turned around to the woman and said, *"Who touched my clothes?"*, and when she responded that it was she who had touched Him, He said, *"I felt virtue go from me. Daughter, thy faith hath made thee whole."* This is the fundamental understanding of "faith healing". The lesson in this is that faith is the taking for granted, with absolute certainty and childlike trust, that assurance that the Creator offers life in perfection and you only have to take it. Faith is simply taking from God what is freely given. As you can see then "faith healing" has nothing whatsoever to do with the healer who only serves as a lightening rod to focus the creative energy until such times as you feel strong enough to act for yourself. Faith is the absolute certainty with which to recognize the Source and to draw from it. Faith to draw and be drawn. And in this way faith activates healing within your body. If you trust that you are able to take from your loving Father in Heaven all that you need to make life good, then that which you need will be given to you and in that process you will be healed.

This of course applies on all the four planes of manifestation, physically, emotionally, mentally, and spiritually. You are simply taking the creative energy from the Source into your own being. And as I just said, until you are strong enough to take that energy for yourself, you may find others who can serve as the lightening rod to have the energy pass through them so that you can receive it through them in the same way that the woman took energy from Jesus Christ. Remember that He, at that time, was pushing his way through a crowd of people. He was being jostled on all sides, and yet he turned around and said, *"Who touched my clothes?"* He was aware of energy being drawn from him.

FORTY-ONE

Q: IS THERE ANY CONNECTION BETWEEN THE CAUSE OF ILL HEALTH AND THE PROCESS OF SELF HEALING?

G: Absolutely, because before you can begin any healing process, you should be able to identify the cause. The cause of your ill-health may be by accident or genetics which you inherited in your three-dimensional form. It may be of energy origin, that is to say, from the emotional and mental attitudes that you have in this life, and it may be spiritual from a past life incident. The effectiveness with which you will be able to heal yourself is greatly enhanced if you first have identified the source. For example, I think it is fairly well accepted today that when one is angry and is constantly expressing anger, a biochemical action takes place in the body. It is possible this biochemical state could cause stones to be formed. So people suffer from stones in the gallbladder and the kidneys. These people have undoubtedly been expressing anger at a very deep level, or holding anger within themselves. So if you are going to get rid of these stones, by all means follow, either the faith healing process, the herbal processes, or medical intervention and get rid of the stones out of the body. But undoubtedly those stones are going to reform, if you still retain the emotion of anger within you. It is a self-perpetuating situation. The stones are a result, symptom, effect or direct product of your anger.

On the other hand it may be that you have no anger within you, but you are creating stones in your kidneys, and when you investigate your environment you find that your water supply is very heavily laden with lime. That lime is accumulated, because possibly your kidneys do not function at an optimum level, and you are not able to flush the lime out of your system. So in that case the stone in your kidney is formed as a direct result of the lime in your water supply.

It may be that within your family line, there is a genetic history of high levels of the chemical in the body which results in the production of stones. That is clearly a case of the genetics within your body, so it is highly likely that you will create stones because of your genetic history.

It may be that you left a previous life carrying an enormous burden of the emotion, anger, and you can truly say, that in this life you are not angry with anyone. Still, that emotion you left a previous life with has not been rebalanced in your energetic field and that energy is still impacting the physical body you are currently utilizing which is causing the production of stones in your body. So you need to look at all the possibilities for the introduction of the disease.

Now I have to mention accident. There are many who will tell you that there is no such thing as accident in the universe. I would put that in a different way. I would say that when God created the manifest universe he programmed the potential for accident into it, because there undoubtedly is accident. Everything is not known. Recently scientists did experiments dealing with the emission of particles in a particle accelerator for an extended period of time and making a computer report of the pattern in which they were emitting. After a period of non-stop running, this machine demonstrated that the particles were emitted in *random* form. This supports the view that there is random chance in the physical universe.

A "Law of Chance" was given to me some time ago by Spirit which says, **"When the conscious will of man advances or delays, through his own interference, the effect of cause in its proper time and place, then chance occurs. It may be said then, that chance occurs as a result of the interference with time."**

So finding the cause of the disease so that you can, perhaps, correct it, will be a matter of looking at your environment, your lifestyle, your genetics, a past life incident or even a chance accident. Everyone is capable of finding the cause if they go within. But let us put it in this way. If you eliminate all other causes and the only one left is a past life, then you can assume that it is a past life and you are dealing with a karmic issue. Karma simply being *The Law of Cause and Effect* as it is expressing itself in peoples lives. Many people have the idea that with any karmic situation, including illness or disease, we have to *live through* it and that is not true. We do not have to *live through* karma. What we have to do is simply identify it, understand it and release it and in so doing, rebalance the energy. We do not have to endure it. I think most people will find that if they have unidentified complaints which do not seem to fit the bill for any of the other reasons and they associate them with a past life incident, even if they are not able to recognize the specific past life involved, they can say to themselves, *"This seems to me to be a of past life origin as I cannot honestly identify it with anything in this life. So on the basis that I may have left a previous life carrying some emotional anger which is now producing this result in my physical body, then I ask that whoever I was angry towards please forgive me for that anger. I myself no longer feel that anger and I wish to neutralize that energy and let it go."* In that instant they are repairing and rebalancing the energy field around them and once that energy field is appropriately rebalanced, the symptoms expressing themselves in the physical body will usually cease to trouble them.

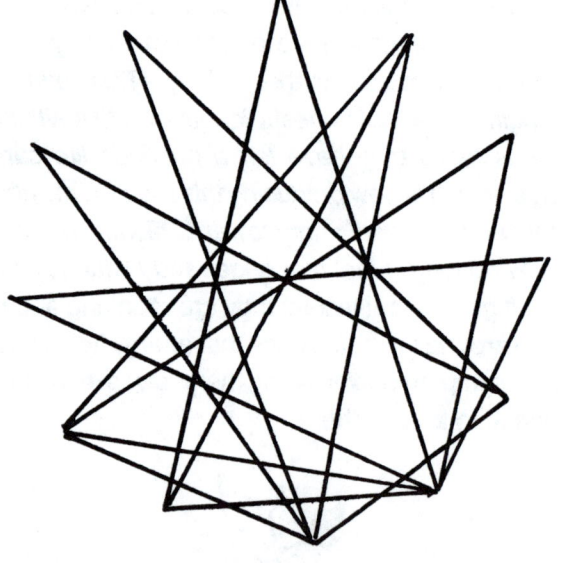

FORTY-TWO

Q: WHY ARE THERE PEOPLE, WHO EVEN THOUGH THEY LIVE THEIR LIVES IN RELATIVE BALANCE, BECOME ILL ANYWAY AND ARE NOT HEALED BY ANY MEANS THEY TRY, INCLUDING PROFESSED FAITH IN THE CREATOR?

G: The first thing I want to say is that the purpose of your existence is *not* to maintain a healthy body. It might be a desirable and helpful thing to do, but that is not the reason you are on the planet. And clearly no matter how balanced a life we have been living, on the physical level most of us are not balanced. We may have achieved mental balance, emotional balance and spiritual balance, but when we are ill we clearly have not achieved physical balance.

Things that are in perfect balance are perfect. A perfect cell is not sick. As to why some one may be sick, could it be because they have been abandoned by the Creator? No. The Creator never abandon's us, *we* abandon the Creator. *We* turn our back on the Creator. So experiencing a chronic or "incurable" illness is never caused by one being abandoned by the Creator. What greater test of faith can someone have than to reach a point where they believe God has abandoned them and yet, still keep faith?

What you choose today creates your tomorrow. However, before you ever come into a lifetime, you make a choice of those situations which you feel will create the optimum environment in which you, as an immortal being, can experience a role in any particular lifetime. It may be that this person's soul felt that the best way in which to grow *spiritually* would be if they lived through illness. Or it may be that they determined before they came to this planet that they were only going to live thirty years. If one has determined that one only needs thirty years of experience on this planet in this particular lifetime, then one has to die of something. What will one die of?

The cause of disease will undoubtedly be because of one of the other areas that we looked at; family genetic history, past-life experiences (karma), or accident. The cause will be rooted in one of the above things. Now there is another issue here that few of us really want to address and is a reality; part of living is *dying*. There is no fate or destiny, except in the sense that our immortal soul-self has a "program of learning" it wishes to fulfill through us.

It also may be, in this case, that our soul has preprogrammed this illness for our own experience and our own growth in some way. And that it is a direct result of our own choosing. Or it may be that we are unfortunate enough to have *mistakenly* contracted this disease which is causing us great pain and suffering. And then one has the choice of whether one will endure that pain and suffering, or not.

Forty-Three

Q: Are you suggesting then that suicide is an option?

G: Yes and no. There are many different forms of suicide. Suicide is to place yourself, of your own free will, in a situation which you know will cause you death. When, in ancient tradition, a virgin threw herself into a volcano to "quiet its anger", when a soldier undertakes an impossible mission, when Christ entered Jerusalem; they all knew death would ensue. They were all "committing suicide", but we call this "sacrifice" because their choices were made in service to others. It is motive which is important.

If you choose to end your life to punish someone else, as the requited lover who says, *"If you leave I'll kill myself"*, then you are greatly misguided. But if you have come to the careful decision that you no longer wish to continue this particular experience then, as you chose to come into this life, so you have the right to choose to leave it. If your intent is pure it follows that your action will also be pure.

There is nothing "natural" about dying from some terrible disease or under the surgeon's knife. It is perfectly natural for you to leave the planet at a time of your choosing, when you feel your work is done. All life is precious. Life is all there is. But when one chooses suicide one is not ending LIFE, simply terminating this physical experience and moving into a different experience of living.

However, in making this choice it seems, according to information I have received from Spirit, that there are certain rules. It is not acceptable, for example, to simply blow your brains out because that action leaves no room for Divine Intervention.

It is acceptable, however, in a Universal sense to, let us say, follow the tradition of early Native American tribes where the elderly sit out on a cold night and freeze to death. Because in that process of ending one's life, there is a space in the time-space continuum in which Divine Intervention can occur. God can interfere with your choice, if you have made a totally mistaken and wrong choice in determining it is time to end your life. You are then allowing that space of time for Divine Intervention to change the circumstances, in this case, either to alter the weather conditions around you or to bring someone to your rescue. So in that sense, suicide simply means self-killing or self-death and as death is only a continuous part of your immortal living, to choose that option is not the great sin many people believe it to be. Dying is truly an option of living, and every living being has the right to determine whether they will live or die.

Please realize that I am by no means an advocate of the wanton destruction of one's life. I am simply saying to you that when all conditions of Universal appropriateness are met it is no sin to choose your own time of departure from this planet.

FORTY-FOUR

Q: WHAT DO YOU HAVE TO SAY ABOUT DOCTOR ASSISTED SUICIDE?

G: I don't know what each doctor's personal motives are, but in a general sense, I would say that by helping those people who have made the decision to end their lives because of extreme circumstances of pain and disease this playing God in the best possible way because the doctor is showing compassion for the suffering of the patient.

Everyone has a right to their own view, and it seems strange to me that so many people cling so tenaciously to life in circumstances which are not bringing them or those around them any apparent joy. But then we can never know what goes on inside someone else's heart, soul and head. This is a personal decision which has to be made by the individual for themselves. I do not support the idea that the medical profession at large should have the authority to determine when you should die. That is playing God in the worst possible sense of expression. But for someone who is assisting people who have made their own decision to die, I have great respect for the doctor's courage in doing so.

FORTY-FIVE

Q: SO IN GENERAL FROM A SPIRITUAL STANDPOINT, IS THE REMOVAL OF LIFE-SUPPORT SYSTEMS APPROPRIATE?

G: Absolutely. The information that I have from Spirit with regard to death is quite simple. They tell me when the heart stops beating and the lungs stop breathing, the patient is dead, in the sense that their soul is free to leave the body.

The measurement that science now uses involving continuing brain activity is entirely dependent upon the oxygen level at the moment of death and the amount of subtle energy that the body is still holding onto at the point of death. And the combination of these factors can continue brain activity long after the individual has actually died and the soul has removed itself from the body. In general people who are being maintained on life-support equipment are not true living beings in that their immortal "self" and soul has departed the body. All you are maintaining is a biochemical body without a living soul in it.

Now in the cases of people who fall into coma for weeks or even months and then revive; so long as the physical body is being kept alive, that silver cord or energy which attaches the spiritual self to the physical self, will not break or separate. In the normal process of death, the person dies and within a space of approximately three days, that energetic thread which connects the spirit to the physical form, thins and separates and the soul or spiritual being is then completely free to go. So long as you maintain the physical body in a physically live state, that is, with movement in the body cells and oxygen, and you are maintaining that life artificially, then the soul will remain attached to that body. If it is a situation where the person comes out of the coma at a later date, that is because the soul has determined it will return into the body to complete whatever it wishes to complete.

As we know from the reports of many who have had so called "near death" experiences, these souls, free of the body, are often asked if they wish to return and/or they must return to the body. This event is an example of Divine Intervention and is a rare and unusual circumstance in modern medicine today.

FORTY-SIX

Q: THERE IS A HINDU SAYING, *"WHEN WORKING WITH ILL PEOPLE, IF YOUR HEART IS PURE, YOU ARE PROTECTED FROM THE SICK INDIVIDUAL'S DISEASE."* IS THIS TRUE?

G: I feel that is a fair statement. Purity of heart is a heart which is expressing unconditional love, which is the love of all things equally. It comes out of the perfect balance of that being. And the foundation of unconditional love is compassion, which has no emotion in it. Compassion is the expression of that unconditional love, which is equal for all, so yes, I would agree with the statement that if you have a pure heart, you will not be affected, because you are not connected in emotional, physical or mental ways to the patient with whom you are dealing. You are only connected by spirit. And, as spirit giving out energy which is unconditional love cannot receive any darkness into itself, so you will not be harmed.

FORTY-SEVEN

Q: MANY PEOPLE SPEAK ABOUT THE SPIRITUAL "WHITE LIGHT" OF PROTECTION. IF ONE IS EXPRESSING UNCONDITIONAL LOVE AND COMPASSION, THEN WILL THIS BALANCE GIVE ONE A VERY LARGE DEGREE, IF NOT TOTAL, PROTECTION?

G: Yes, but protection from what? Jesus the Nazarene was God made manifest, but that did not protect him from the scourge and Crucifixion. The Pharaoh Akahnaton was a Hathor and came to this planet to be a teacher thousands of years before Christ. He brought the concept of the *One living God* and devoted his whole life to service to the Source, but was not protected from being driven insane by the poisons of the priests. So when you are talking about protection, you have to ask, *"Protection from what?"* There is a phrase that was given to me by a friend. *"We must learn to stand in the shadow of darkness without being affected by that darkness."* That is to say that we must be able to be involved in all the dark things that occur on this planet, including homelessness and disease, and not allow our light to be dimmed. That is a matter of our attitude and our faith, where we stand.

The idea of putting "white light" around you is a way of reminding yourself to be conscious of your energy field and to be conscious of that connection with your Creator which is a constant flow from the Creator to you of pure unconditional love. One might perceive unconditional love as white light of the perfect original form. When you are encased in that perfect love of the Creator then the things of this world are not going to harm you. But if you are attached to the things of this world, then through your attachments, you can and may be harmed.

In the matter of health and healing, you must first ask yourself, where are you focused? If you are focused on your body and on the things of this physical world, then it is in that body that you will have your concerns. It is in that body you will need to practice your healing. And it is in that body that you will experience all the things that you experience here. Better that you have less concern for your body and more concern for the healing of your immortal soul. For if you heal the body, you only heal the body and the body will die. And one day your body will be returned to dust. But if you heal your soul then you are healing your immortal self and you will live forever.

FORTY-EIGHT

Q: WHAT HAPPENED DURING THE CRUCIFIXION OF CHRIST THAT INVOLVED HEALING?

G: Christ was God made manifest within a human being. He was the ultimate demonstration of the potential of all human beings. Many people work on the balancing of their chakras. The goal in life is to achieve perfect balance. When you have all your chakras in balance as a result of having all your life in balance, then all those colors of the rainbow that emit from chakras culminate in the white light which is then emitted from the crown chakra. The unconditional love of God may be expressed as the perfect white light. That is the "stuff" of Creation.

Throughout all our lives, we are connected to the Creator and we are taking from the Creator that love — that white light — into our being for our maintenance. When we become perfect as Christ was perfect, then we are united with the Creator and then we are emitting white light and no longer taking the light. We are *giving* light instead of *taking* it. In that process of union with the Creator, we again become connected with all things. When Christ was crucified, He, as God made manifest in man and united with God, was connected to all beings. In an act of complete love and obedience to the Will of God He laid aside his own will and offered His life upon the cross. This was to be followed by the Resurrection, as a means of demonstrating immortality to man, as means of letting man know that his immortality was possible and real. In order to demonstrate that, he had first to die then be "resurrected". In that act of sacrifice of self in obedience to the Will of God, Christ was perfectly joined to God and so connected energetically to all living souls. In that moment He, Christ, was able to serve as the lightening rod of humanity and neutralize all destructive energy harbored in the souls of mankind. Man, from that moment was washed clean and given a fresh start.

So the Crucifixion was a total healing of all the souls on the planet. He then went through the process of resurrection. He showed himself to people and said, *"Look this is what you can do! You can have immortal life. This is the real potential for every single one of you!"* And from that moment we then had the option to "start over" and get it right. But when we look at our world 2000 years later and we see man's inhumanity to man, clearly we haven't got it right—we haven't obeyed the rules and we are once again in a state of soul *im*perfection.

Now there are individuals within humanity who *are* getting it right within this lifetime. Many, many people are becoming conscious human beings. They are igniting that Divine spark within their own souls. They are becoming aware and in that process of awareness, they are making rapid progress toward the next evolutionary step for humanity.

FORTY-NINE

Q: ARE WE ALL ACTUALLY CAPABLE OF GIVING VARYING DEGREES OF HEALING LIGHT?

G: Every time you smile at someone and your smile reaches from your eyes as well as your mouth, you are giving light to someone else. The eyes are truly the windows of the soul. They take the light in and they emit the light out. As any true healer will tell you, the work is not done by them when they lay on their hands, the work is done by where they look — by where they focus their gaze — because when the Divine Light of healing flows through them it enters directly from the Divine Source through the crown chakra and is emitted directly from the pupils of their eyes.

The part about putting hands on and touching the sick person is, if you like, the showmanship which goes with the process. Most people being healed need to feel that something is being done, so that simple act of looking at someone is usually not enough. The actual healing is done through the physical eyes and also through the third eye. Those three beams come together in triangulated form and create something which is akin to a laser beam. A healing beam is like a laser which comes from the third eye, the two physical eyes and closes down onto that triangle form to a single beam that is bright blue. That is a true beam of healing of Divine energy coming through as healing light. If you go and stand out in the sun and expose your body to the rays of the sun, (although with the ozone depletion at this time, most of us are not well enough adjusted to deal with the additional radiation) when you expose your body to sunlight, to pure full spectrum lighting, you are assisting in the evolution of your immortal soul. This is because you are taking more light into yourself at the physical level. So whether you are approaching your spiritual growth from the internal soul expanding outwards, or whether you are working for the growth of your soul from the outside in, doesn't really matter because both processes help.

One of the greatest ways to assist our soul growth is to eat raw carrots or drink carrot juice. This is because of the very low dyne level which allows it to permeate the semi-permeable membranes of the cells and literally clean them out. By cleaning them out, by removing the garbage that collected within the cells themselves of the physical body, you are leaving more space that can be filled with light. The process of spiritual evolution and enlightenment is balance on all four levels. The physical body becomes filled with light. The emotional body becomes filled with light. The mental body becomes filled with light and then the spiritual being becomes filled with light as all things are brought into balance. This is a very real thing. That is why you have to attend to all levels. It is not something you do at one level and then forget about the rest. If God determined that we should manifest in the three-dimensional reality on four planes, then we must attend to all four planes.

FIFTY

Q: DISCUSS THE MANIPULATION OF ENERGY.

G: The manipulation of energy. Let us first remind you of the two rules governing this universe, and specifically, the one which inherently forbids interference with the lifestream of another. Therefore, *any* form of manipulation, whether it is in the physical world or the energetic world, is totally inappropriate for an evolving soul. We must never manipulate the energy of others. Having said that, I would add that while manipulation of the energy of others without their knowledge is always inappropriate, there are times when, in the process of healing work, people ask that their energy field be worked on, or manipulated in some way to improve their healing. In that way they are giving authority and permission to the healer to manipulate their energy field. While this then is acceptable, it represents hazard for the healer, because the healer must be aware that in the same way as when you speak, you may be speaking the words of a high spiritual being but you are nonetheless responsible for the words which come out of your mouth. It is the same when you manipulate or work with someone's energy field, even though they are asking you to do it, you still have responsibility karmicly for the results which ensue from your work. So the manipulation of energy in that sense could be acceptable, but also represents possible hazard for the worker.

In regards to massage therapists, if the intent is to work on your physical body, that is where the impact is going to be. It will have some effect on your energetic field, but that is not what they are directly working on.

A good massage therapist, by relieving muscle tension and restoring healthy circulation, can greatly assist the release of "blocks" in one's energy field.

FIFTY-ONE

Q: IF ONE WERE TO GO AND HAVE ENERGY WORK DONE ON THEMSELVES, WHAT WOULD INITIALLY BE THE MOST IMPORTANT INFORMATION THEY MUST KNOW ABOUT THAT PERSON?

G: It is very difficult to make a hard and fast rule about this, so I am simply sharing my opinion here. From my perspective the most important thing you need to ask the energy worker is, *"Do you see the energy, either clairvoyantly with the third eye, or with the physical eyes? Do you actually see the energy you are working with?"* It has been my experience to meet people who have had energy work done, by practioners who could not see what they were doing, and the energy, either auric, etheric or both has been moved to one side and out of alignment. I have seen this on numerous occasions. So I think that it is very important that the practioner you are working with can assure you that they can actually see what they are doing. I don't think you would want to go and have your appendix out by a surgeon who is blind. To me it is most important that you don't have the *geometry* of your energetic field manipulated, altered and disturbed by someone who cannot see what they are doing.

Fifty-Two

Q: WHAT QUALIFIES AN INDIVIDUAL TO BE WORTHY AND CAPABLE OF OFFERING HEALING OR SPIRITUAL GUIDANCE TO ANY OTHER HUMAN BEING BESIDES THEMSELVES?

G: There are only two qualifications required. Total unconditional love *of* God and Man and total humility *before* God and Man. I would say that the key to knowing one's intent would be if one uses the words; "*I want* to heal", "*I want* to save", "*I want* to raise the consciousness", "*I want* to help"...If one looks at one's "*I wants*", one will see that all one wishes to do is in the expression of one's own ego.

Fifty-Three

Q: Is THERE ANY WAY THAT PEOPLE CAN EVALUATE THEIR URGE TO BE OF SERVICE TO HELP THEM DETERMINE WHETHER THEY ARE TRULY BEING DIRECTED BY GOD'S WILL, OR WHETHER IT IS COMING OUT OF THEIR OWN EGO.

G: One could try answering the questionnaire below, but I only know one man who could answer "Yes", and His perfection would never allow Him to answer. Most of us must just do our best to be humble and accepting of what God puts before us.

QUESTIONNAIRE: Questions to ask yourself to determine ego or God's will:

1. Do I believe I am perfect?
2. Do I believe I am perfectly balanced emotionally?
3. Do I believe I am perfectly balanced mentally?
4. Do I believe I am perfectly balanced spiritually?
5. Do I believe I am perfectly balanced physically?

If we could live the statement, *"Thy will be my will and my will be Thy will"*, then we could be reasonably sure God was directing our life and service.

Another way that one might verify whether one is following God's direction or one's own ego direction, would be to ask yourself, *"If God asked me to go out and serve by healing the planet, does this fill me with joy?"* And the answer presumably would be "Yes". Then ask yourself the question, *"If God asks me to go and scrub latrines as a volunteer in a homeless center, would this fill me equally with joy?"* And if, when answering that question, you have any sense of repulsion or distaste for the work, then you can be sure that your impulses are not coming from the Creator, but are coming from your own ego. Because in fact, anything that God asked you to do, would fill you with joy. To the evolved soul, the more humbling the task, the greater the joy will be.

Fifty-Four

Q: From the nature of the questionnaire, it sounds as if none of us would qualify or be worthy to be of service because if we were to answer these questions honestly, how could we say we were perfect in every way?

G: That is absolutely true. I think that it is an essential part of our growth and understanding to realize that none of us are worthy. Remember John the Baptist? When Jesus came to the River Jordan, and presented himself for Baptism, John said to Him, and I paraphrase, "*Lord I am not even worthy to unlatch your sandals, never mind to be baptizing you.*" I think that if we reach the point of knowing that of *ourselves* we are not worthy to heal, to teach, to raise the consciousness of any other living being, that we are hardly even capable of dragging ourselves along, and that without *God's Grace*, we are capable of nothing. When we reach that level of understanding and humility, then we are truly detached from our ego. Only then are we fit to be used as tools in service to God and man.

So then in order to "pass" this test, your answers would all be "No"? Isn't that the paradox of the life of the spirit, that in order to succeed, we must fail? If we are ever to become worthy, we must first recognize our total unworthiness. It is not by our own judgment that we are deemed worthy, but by the judgment of God. He will decide if we are worthy or not. And then He will place the work before us which is appropriate for us to do.

It will no longer be a matter of us saying, "*I want* to do this". It will be a simple case that we do it.

FIFTY-FIVE

Q: DOES THE FOOD WE EAT IN ANY WAY AFFECT OUR SPIRITUAL DEVELOPMENT?

G: If you are a healthy person within your appropriate weight range, the best thing for you to eat is whatever your body tells you it wants. Your body is a VERY self-aware, complex chemical factory and it knows, to the smallest pinch of salt, exactly what it needs to function efficiently. Try ASKING your body what it wants before each meal—you'll be surprised how quickly you get the knack of recognizing its requests.

We all are familiar with the idea of the pregnant woman with odd dietary cravings. Keep in mind you are now "pregnant". You are in process of transmutation of cellular structure, giving birth to the New Enlightened You and as you go through this process, you, like the pregnant woman, may find your body craving foods you do not usually eat. Trust your body and comply with its requests.

In regard to special food, diets, etc.; IF you are spiritually prepared then certain foodstuffs may be of great assistance to you. However, if you are NOT spiritually prepared, no amount of special food or diet will alter that state of preparedness. Put simply, eating fresh fruit and vegetables won't make you spiritual, but if you are spiritual you may well wish to eat of fresh fruits and vegetables. Keep in mind, a true Master transmutes all to his good and will gratefully accept whatever is offered for sustenance by the giver.

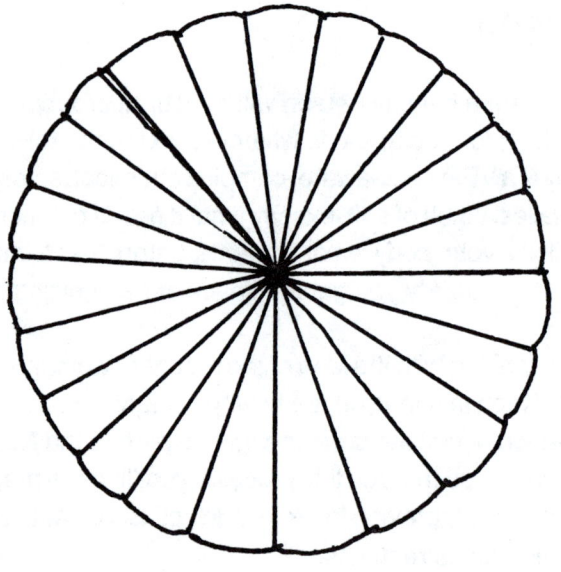

FIFTY-SIX

Q: HOW IMPORTANT IS FORGIVENESS FOR THE DEVELOPMENT OF SOUL PERFECTION?

G: Someone once said to me, *"Love is for giving"*. So if we are in the process of giving love into any situation, it naturally follows that we are forgiving anything that is, from our perspective, detrimental to us in that situation. It is very important that we have this giving, loving and forgiving nature for the development of our soul. It is just as important that we keep in mind that when we look at any situation and feel that we need to forgive, we are making a judgment on the "right" and "wrong" of that situation. And maybe it is we who need forgiving. It seems to me that we would be better served in looking to that which we need pardoned in ourselves, rather than paying too much attention to that which we perceive we need to forgive in others. After all anything which we forgive in others is only our perception, and therefore, we are only forgiving a perception. Whilst this may have a wonderful healing effect on our emotional body, it will do little more than satisfy our ego in the spiritual sense, especially if our perception was mistaken in the first place. Which of us has "all knowledge" with which to perceive the "rights" and "wrongs" of any situation? No, better we assume responsibility for our own actions and ask forgiveness when we are in error and make no attempt to judge the "rights" and "wrongs" of another.

"Without love of self we have no compassion, with only love of self we have no God."

Fifty-Seven

Q: Isn't this process of determining what we will forgive in others a means by which we work toward balance with people and situations in an effort to achieve oneness?

G: No, certainly not. This is a very misleading perception. There is only one "Oneness" and that is the oneness of God. And God in His wisdom created this planet with many differences. For example look at all the differences among animals, nations, people and even the varied and different climates which manifest on the planet. We do not have to forgive someone for being different from us. We simply have to accept their difference. Once we accept all the differences then all those differences are united in the whole.

Fifty-Eight

Q: WILL YOU SPEAK ON THE SUBJECT OF PRAYER. HOW MUST WE PRAY IN ORDER TO ASSIST US IN THE PERFECTION OF OUR SOULS?

G: When the disciples asked Jesus to tell them how to pray, He gave them the Lord's Prayer. It is simple and to the point. A way of viewing the Lord's Prayer which will enhance your spiritual growth is not, as you are saying it, to relate it to your material life, but to relate it instead to your soul.

First there is the acknowledgment of the Creator, *"Our Father who art in heaven"*. As you say this rejoice in the fact that Jesus invited you to claim the same Father as He Himself and so named Himself your brother.

"Hallowed be thy name". Honor the sacred name of your Father.

"Thy kingdom come, Thy will be done on earth as it is in heaven". Here, think of the kingdom of your soul and be conscious of asking God's will to be worked within it.

"Give us this day our daily bread". Instead of allowing your mind the thought of "my work, employment, my means of sustenance and my physical survival," think of your daily bread as being the flow of light, of love, the creative energy from the Creator flowing into you. That is your daily bread, the food for your soul, rather than the food for your body.

"Forgive us our trespasses as we forgive those who trespass against us". A simple statement of release and as you ask to be forgiven, so also think of the things you need to forgive. On the day that you can find nothing that you feel you need to forgive in others because nothing anyone has done to you offends you, on that day you will know the feeling of real humility. Then you have an indication that your soul is making progress. When you examine a day in your life and you truly feel that no one has wronged you, no matter what has happened, because you accept full responsibility for being the cause of all that comes into your life, and if someone has wronged you, you accept with humility that you must have sometime done something to deserve it, then you are able to completely release any sense of the need to forgive anyone else. Then you are beginning to truly learn humility.

"Lead us not into temptation". A simple request, acknowledging to the Father that your soul is weak and easily tempted, to protect you from those temptations which you are not yet strong enough to resist.

"Deliver us from evil". Save our souls from being exposed to that which would be damaging to us and would draw us back into our own weaknesses.

"For Thine is the Kingdom, the Power and the Glory, forever and ever, Amen." The Kingdom, the Power and the Glory being the Three-Fold Flame within your own soul which truly belongs to the Creator.

That is the most simple and straight forward prayer. If you focus your attention on your soul, instead of your material life, then you are making a prayer which is truly going to connect your soul with the Divine.

The danger with prayer, especially when it is a long convoluted prayer, is that most people end up having a conversation with themselves, not with God. You find yourself praying and in the process of prayer, you begin to justify and begin to excuse and become completely entangled in your own intelligence and ego, so it ceases to be prayer.
If you wish to offer prayer which will lift your soul nearer the Creator,

better you only offer one word, but offer that word in complete love, humility and total abandonment of your entire being to the love of God. If you only cry, *"Help me"*, that prayer is going to be heard. If, like the Pharisee, you stand on the street corner and voice loud prayers, it is very possible God will turn a deaf ear.

Your Notes

Fifty-Nine

Q: IF YOU PRAY, FOR EXAMPLE, *FOR* ANOTHER HUMAN BEING OR *FOR* WORLD PEACE, ARE THESE WORTHY AND EFFECTIVE PRAYERS?

G: All prayer is worthy. The fact that you are praying is better than not praying. Because at least by praying you are acknowledging the existence of the Creator. If you are doing nothing else, you are doing that. As to praying for other people, prayer offered for others is always good provided that you end all prayers with the words, *"Thy will be done"*, or something similar, so that you, yourself, are not determining what is best for someone else. It is fine to pray for world peace, if you say, *"Thy will be done."* But you know, if everyone prayed for peace in his own heart there would BE world peace.

This question reminds me of something Hermes once said to me a long time ago. I was asking for insight on a difficult situation in which I was only marginally involved and he said to me, *"Go pull weeds in your own back yard."*

Your Notes

Sixty

Q: Is there any specific way that one must meditate to meditate successfully?

G: It is what works for you. For some people one specific form of meditation is better than another.

Meditation, I prefer to think of, as quiet time. A time when you go within the silence and completely exclude all exterior thoughts, words, and deeds. Be focused only on the God essence within you. Meditation is a time when you can come face to face with the Christ within your soul. When you are talking about group meditation practices, for example, when somebody *leads* a meditation, that is never meditation because you are listening to what they are saying, and/or listening to music. You are not meditating, you are listening.

The requisites of meditation are solitude and going within your own soul. Music is not necessary. Some people find music helpful to move them into the state of meditation, but those who are proficient will tell you that once they get into that state of meditation where they are moving into alpha and theta brain waves, they no longer hear the music. Meditation, of itself, is going into the silence. The silence within where you can make connection with your own soul, and connection with the Divine. It is often a meditational practice to focus all of the energy of the body into the region of the third eye. A practitioner in meditation focused on the progress of their soul is going to take all that collected energy down from the third eye into the heart chakra. The focus of energy is going to be at the base of the heart which is the seat of the soul.

For myself, it is a rarity for me to actually sit and do a specific meditation. It is something I seldom do. I discovered that that was because, having been born clairvoyant, I have never known a time when I couldn't connect with Spirit at one level or another. Therefore, in my life, I am either *one hundred percent* focused on the activities that I am involved in my normal physical life, or I am meditating. It is unusual for me to experience that space of time where I am doing nothing physically, and my head is filled with trivia. It's not a virtue on my part, I just happened to be born that way. So for me, meditation is fifty percent of my life. Fifty percent of the time I am physically doing something, fifty percent of the time I am connecting with Spirit at some level either through my work or during quiet time. It often happens that a real communion with spirit occurs when the body is fully occupied in some mindless task, such as housework or walking. For me, weeding the garden is a wonderful time of meditation. We must all try our best to set aside some time each day exclusively for God.

SIXTY-ONE

Q: WHAT ABOUT CONTEMPLATION?

G: Contemplation is a parallel track to meditation. In meditation we open ourselves to many things. In contemplation we concentrate on one thing only. If that which we are concentrating upon is material, this may be referred to as cognitive contemplation. But if our focus of concentration is upon a spiritual matter, as for example, the meaning of love, then this may be termed non-cognitive contemplation.

In order to contemplate it is necessary to go into a deep state of physical relaxation. An ideal position for this is the Lotus position because this keeps the spine straight and the chakras properly aligned. Once you are fully relaxed you must then place your attention on the object or thought you wish to contemplate and allow your awareness to absorb and be absorbed by it to the exclusion of all else. It is best to begin your practice by choosing an object in the physical world on which to place your attention—a pebble will do very well. Then once you have a sense of what you are doing in a total awareness experience you will be ready for some non-cognitive contemplation. If you begin by contemplating on the more wide ranging subjects, such as "love", "perfection", or "wisdom", you may find it hard to keep your mind on the subject until you have had a little practice. But keep at it, as you will find the awareness that such contemplation awakens in you will be very rewarding.

Your Notes

Sixty-Two

Q: IS THERE A SPECIAL MEDITATION WE MAY PRACTICE WHICH WE WILL ALLOW US TO CONNECT WITH THIS "CHALICE OF OUR SOULS"?

G: Yes. You may care to try the following meditational form. Place a veil over your head and draw it around your face. By this physical act, you are demonstrating your intent to close out this world. Then say aloud, *"Oh mighty and great God, essence of infinite mind, we give thee thanks for this day and we come humbly before you seeking your presence."* Now focus your mind on your heart. Seek out that small space within the human heart where dwells the eternal flame. The flame of power, wisdom and love. See that sacred flame flicker and grow. Feel its warmth heating and healing your heart, filling you with charity and compassion. Let the immortal flame rise up and engulf you. Let it flow through your body, mind and spirit burning out all disease. Know this flame of Creation, the God Force within, and fear it not. Let the fingers of this holy fire reach out now and touch the hearts of those close to you. Of those you love and those you despise and let all hatred and discomfort be devoured by the flame. Let your soul be consumed in the fire of love that you may be at one with the Father. In that place be still. Listen to the voice within which speaks to you from the midst of the flame and be at one with God.

So often when we meditate, we raise our consciousness to the area of the third eye. And then we think in terms of expanding upward and outward, reaching and stretching for something beyond ourselves. And in that way we can have many wonderful, uplifting and enlightening experiences. We can communicate with Spirit. We can touch the wonders of the Cosmos. The whole Creation is there for us to experience. But if you would know your God, then go within. Take your mind, your consciousness, your whole being down into that place in the heart. For it is there that you can come face to face with yourself and with your Creator. This is not an easy journey, for in the process of passing through yourself and through your heart, you come face to face with all the areas of mistakes of your own life. But when you have the humility to accept your nothingness, when you can abandon yourself to the eternal light within, then you can truly know your God.

Sixty-Three

Q: Will you explain the difference between knowledge and wisdom?

G: To acquire knowledge we must first have information about a subject. We then take that information and we digest it, meditate on it, think about it, use our God-given reasoning ability, and we might even pray about it. When we have thoroughly understood all that information and it is clear to us intellectually, then we have knowledge. What knowledge does for us is help us to broaden the scope of our questions. We can then take that knowledge down into our souls and receive enlightenment by the Grace of God in respect to that knowledge. Then we have wisdom.

Perfect wisdom only comes through the union with Divine Intelligence and is an inner knowing which is beyond understanding. We receive it through the language of light of which there are no expressions through our human intellect.

Sixty-Four

Q: Speak about sexuality as it relates to our spirituality and the perfection of our souls.

G: The act of procreation is the nearest we can come to copying God's creation of life. It is a creative force, par excellence, by which man may perpetuate himself. From time immemorial the dark forces have used this powerful creative energy to aid their own purposes here on earth. Today their are many advocates for "sexual" energy being used as a path toward enlightenment. And there are those who will even say living in a certain way will ensure sex at a "higher" or "cosmic" level. On the one hand it may be true that the sexual act between *spiritually* motivated people may well create a more powerful energetic exchange to take place between them, but the other side of that coin is that when they are *spiritually* motivated they will have transmuted physical sexual desire into the deeper desire of participation in creation through the union with God. The sexual act is by its very nature, at least in part, an act of self-gratification and self-gratification is never going to be the concern of the spiritually evolved.

Q: Please discuss Homosexuality.

G: As it was shown to me, there are three distinct energy fields identifying homosexuals. As these fields were being shown to me by Spirit, this is the information which I was given. First, there are a very small number who do not choose to be, but are, males existing in female bodies and females existing in male bodies due to a chromosomal error.

These people see the world very differently from most of us and should be helped in every way possible to deal with their circumstance. Secondly, there is a group who, of their own will, choose to act out a variety of sexual perversions in their lives. These people are both sick and dangerous and should be treated as such.

Lastly, and by far the largest group today especially among the under 40-year-olds, are those highly evolved beings, who, on their path of enlightenment had long ago passed beyond carnal desire or any need to participate in a three-dimensional experience. These beings have chosen to return to the planet to assist during the transition. Unfortunately, many, upon arrival here have forgotten who they are and why they came. But they do return with an awareness which tells them they do *not* wish to involve themselves in the conflict of male/female relationships. Like all people craving companionship, many of them have turned to the homosexual lifestyle for love and sharing. The energy field of these beings is so bright and unique as to be unmistakable to any "seer". It is a great service to these beings and to humanity, whom they came to serve, if they can in any way be helped to see and remember their intended purpose.

Each person must take responsibility for his own actions in life, whatever they are. I am suggesting that if you profess to be walking a *spiritual* path, there are some useful guidelines pertaining to all relationships: 1. Christ told his disciples to, *"Love one another as I have loved you."* 2. Shared love is always "good", it is the shared *acts* which we use to express love which we must sometimes question. 3. The exchange of bodily fluids creates a karmic link between two people. That energy will need to be balanced at some point. In this regard I doubt if those highly evolved souls who, through forgetfulness, are choosing a particular lifestyle at this time, would be very happy with themselves if they find they are once again bound to the three-dimensional experience in the future to rebalance that energy. Indeed this is true for *all* of us when expending our sexual energy. The inappropriate use of sexual energy is without doubt an exceedingly powerful karmic trap

Q: What is an appropriate use of sexual energy?

G: As the physical expression of a *genuine* feeling of love between two people and for the procreation of the species.

Sixty-Five

Q: PLEASE DESCRIBE WHAT LIFE BETWEEN LIVES MAY BE LIKE AND WHAT CHOICES WE ARE ALLOWED TO EXERCISE BEFORE ENTERING A NEW BODY.

G: We are in a cycle of approximately 50,000 years when we are completing a series of reincarnations upon this particular planet. We will find that between each of those lives, we move into the astral plane.

The astral plane itself is an energetic band surrounding the planet and attached to the planet's magnetic field. Life in the astral plane will in many ways have the appearances, senses and feelings of life on this plane. This is because that which attaches us to the cycles of reincarnation is emotion. As we experience emotion on this plane, so we will continue to experience emotion in the astral plane. In the astral plane we will be able to consult with our spiritual guides, teachers and more highly evolved beings. These beings will enable us to review the life previously experienced in order to learn all that we need to learn and to recognize those areas where we were moving forward in our spiritual growth and those areas where we were holding ourselves back. In preparation for the next lifetime we will, with the aid of our spiritual counselors, prepare an outline plan of action. This is our soul's preprogramming before we enter into a new body and is the nearest that we have to a thread of destiny in any one lifetime.

For example if we need to learn the lessons of unconditional love, then it is possible that we may set up in advance a series of experiences which we will live through which will pressure us in some way to develop that ability of loving unconditionally within ourselves. This concept is the foundation stone of the idea that we are responsible for everything that ever happens to us. In order to insure the optimum environment for the fulfillment of our programming for our next lifetime we will, with the aid of Spirit, seek out and choose that family, environment and genetic background which will most likely enable us to fulfill our soul's programming. The amount of choice we have in this matter is almost entirely dependent upon how well we had utilized our energy in the previous life. So those who use their energy well will have the first choice in the optimum environment for the future. Whilst those who did not use their energy well will, of course, simply have to take any life experience which happens to be available to them at the time that they need it. This may or may not afford them the most ideal environment for their experiences and growth.

It has been shown to me by Spirit that when a soul enters a new body, that soul has a period up to one year in which to determine whether or not it is able to fulfill its programming for that lifetime. So in the infant body, it has the capability of stopping both breath and heartbeat in order to speedily end that incarnation. My understanding is that this is a God-given right of every soul to choose whether it will fulfill its intent in a lifetime, or not. As controlling both heart rate and breathing is a well known means of exiting this planet among adepts and aborigines, it is not surprizing that the new soul should retain this knowledge during the first year of life and have the ability to exercise it. And I believe that many of those infant deaths labeled "Cot" deaths are in fact small souls choosing not to complete the lifetime that they had started.

There is a "purgatory" existing in the astral plane. It is called the Hall of Memories to which we go after death. It is there that we can review the life just ended, and, with clear vision, see our "mistakes". Can you imagine what "hell" it will be to suffer the embarrassment of viewing our every thought, word and deed? There is an old expression which says, *"If you can't face your action on tomorrow's front page, don't do it."* Good advice.

Sixty-Six

Q: Speak about astral travel and dreams.

G: Journeys undertaken in the astral form while the physical body is at rest or sleeping are called "astral travel" or "astral projection". Everyone goes on astral journeys or projections, during the natural sleep time. I often think that it is not so much that the body needs sleep, but the spirit needs a break from the confines of the physical body. Sleeping astral projection may not always be under the control of the sleeper and recollection of experiences encountered on the astral plane will be in the form of remembered dreams, although many people do not even remember their dreams.

I am shown that the actual projected experiences occur during the deep part of sleep and that the REM (rapid eye movement) stage is when the mind/spirit is feeding its experiences back into the brain. Much of the confusion found in dreams occurs at this stage because it is necessary to translate the experiences into a form the brain is familiar with in some way. Not all dreams are memories of a projection but it is quite easy to learn to differentiate between a projection and hyper-activity of the brain itself which may be intruding on sleep.

Astral travels may be undertaken with the conscious control of the traveller and this is a technique which can be learned. There are many good books teaching various methods of astral projection, but my own feeling is that this is not an experience to be undertaken lightly or by the beginning student as, in my view, a firm grounding in the principles of metaphysics and a solid spiritual foundation is very necessary before such an undertaking.

When projecting our astral body out beyond our physical body the two remain connected by the "silver cord". This cord comprises of a myriad living, vibrating particles. It is endless and unbreakable and during projection may be seen as a string of silvery blue light. After death of the physical body and departure of the spiritual body the silver cord thins and separates. There is a tradition which says that this separation of the cord takes three days and this may be the reason why many do not bury their dead until the third day. It, of course, also coincides with the Resurrection of Christ on the third day.

Dreams can be of great use to you as a means of learning whilst your body sleeps, but first you must recognize the different types of dreams. For our purposes, we can think of dreams as falling into two categories: First, those dreams which are as a result of hyper-activity of the brain, maybe due to some event experienced during the day or seen on television. These dreams either tend to be a replay of events experienced or a complete mixing of several experiences, making no sense. It is also possible in this variety of dream to "program" the brain with some problem you are having and find that the brain will work on it in the night and solve it for you by morning.

Second are the dreams we are primarily interested in and which I refer to as "true dreaming". These "dreams" are sleeping astral projections and are undertaken by everyone during normal sleep periods. In order to benefit from these projections you must first learn to control them and the way to do this is to identify an object, such as your ring, and then, each time during the dream that you feel the dream slipping away you can refocus on your ring to stabilize the situation. It takes a little practice, but it can be done and once you have this level of control during your dream you can then decide where you wish to go; perhaps to a teacher on a higher plane, or to visit a friend who lives far from you. However you choose to use your nights the essential thing is to keep good records of your experiences, so write them down as soon as you arise. You will soon find it easy to distinguish between the two types of dreams outlined here and you can receive great benefits from the second type.

Sixty-Seven

Q: DISCUSS WHAT THE RELATIONSHIP OF COLORS IS TO OUR SPIRITUALITY.

G: Colors are the way in which certain vibrations express themselves to our vision. They are a recognizable link showing relationship between a specific manifestation and the spiritual energy that manifestation is expressing. For example, red is the color associated with the planet Mars and Mars is the planet of physical energy. In this way colors are recognized to be associated with certain attributes. The following list is a generally accepted interpretation of the spiritual attributes of the colors seen in the human aura:

White:	Spiritual strength, purity, power and truth.
Red:	Will power, energy, strength and leadership.
Rose:	Unconditional love, childlike love.
Gold:	Mystical power, universal love, success, concentration.
Pale Gold:	Philosophic understanding.
Orange:	Joy, friendship, attraction, strong love.
Green:	Fertility, healing, service.
Blue:	Truth, wisdom, honesty.
Violet:	Royal power, wisdom, protection, spiritual gifts.
Black:	Evil or as a shield from evil. Secrets and hidden things.

When working with colors keep in mind that at the heart of all colors there is the core of white light which is itself the expression of all the colors combined.

SIXTY-EIGHT

Q: EXPLAIN WHAT THE AURIC FIELD IS AND WHAT THE ETHERIC AND CAUSAL BODIES ARE.

G: The aura is a multi-colored living, vibrating field of energy surrounding every living thing. Around people it forms a luminous egg shape and may stretch for as much as five or six feet from the body. People are very sensitive to any invasion of their auric field. Have you ever had "goose bumps" when someone you disliked stood next to you? Each individual has his own rate of vibration in his auric field. When you meet someone that you instantly dislike, one explanation may be that his rate of vibration is very different from yours and that the two vibratory rates do not harmonize.

As you move along on your path toward spiritual perfection, you will raise your rate of vibration and this, in turn, will make you increasingly uncomfortable with those vibrating at a lower rate. Just remember, one is not better than another, only different; in the same way that when two men are walking along a path in single file, the one in the lead is neither better nor worse than the one following, just simply at a different point on the path. As one's rate of vibration increases the colors of the aura will brighten and clarify and they may even change completely.

The etheric body is the field of energy around us which exactly duplicates the physical body, projecting anywhere from half and inch to several inches out from our physical body. It looks silvery blue/grey in color, not unlike cigarette smoke, and can be photographed using Kirlian photography. It is also quite easy to learn to see the etheric for yourself.

The energy of which it comprises is found around all living things and will dissipate shortly after death. It is the physical nervous energy you are constantly giving off from your body, especially the palms of your hands, the soles of your feet and the top of your head. A study of the etheric is well worthwhile as you can learn to conserve this energy, return it to the body and draw upon it in times of need. It was shown to me many years ago by an English healer that when the etheric is maintaining its "glow" you can take this as a sign that the person still has time on their side and that they may be healed of their sickness. Unfortunately, when the etheric shows only as a dull dark grey or black line close to the body, then this may be an indication that the patient has completed his or her life cycle for the present and healing, whilst relieving pain and suffering, is unlikely to effect a cure or recovery.

The Causal body is the inner body of incarnation through which we absorb our experience of the physical world. It is not necessary to understand the concept of the causul body, just know that you have an inner core which is registering and transmitting to your "higher" self all that you are and are becoming.

Sixty-Nine

Q: Please speak about the purpose of a "personal guide". Is this guide assigned or self-chosen?

G: We can all choose to ask for guidance from God, Christ, from any of the highly evolved beings whom we choose. In addition to this it seems more that you are chosen rather than you do the choosing in the sense of a personal spiritual guide. As your awareness grows and expands, so will the teachers assigned to you have wider and more far-ranging knowledge which is appropriate to your level of spiritual growth at that time. In this way then you will have guidance from both those who are assigned to you, or have chosen you, and those whom you have chosen.

As to purpose; "guides" are teachers for us. At first your personal guide may have given you all the answers you asked for, guiding and directing your footsteps each step of the way. As you mature spiritually the guidance you receive will, more and more, take the form of ideas and questions for you to ponder. You will also usually find as you go along that you *ask* less of your guide, especially on personal matters. This is because, as time and experience develop the trust and communication between you, you will notice that that which you *need* to know is always made available to you, even without asking. Your guide will never interfere in your life or decision making process without your permission.

Years ago I made it a habit, each morning, to say to Spirit, *"Show me what I need to know"*, and then leave it up to my spiritual teachers to present my lessons to me. This has worked well for me over the years and you may like to try it.

Seventy

Q: What are the Akashic Records, their purpose and who has access to them?

G: The Akashic Record is a frequency of consciousness throughout all of Creation on which is stored the records of everything that ever was or ever will be; past, present and probable future. The Akashic Records are similar to radio waves in that one may transmit a radio frequency and many hours later in a distant place, this message may be received by having a receiver capable of tuning into that frequency. There is nothing complex about the Akashic Records. They are simply a frequency storage system.

Anyone attaining that level of frequency within their own vibrations which allows them to harmonize with the frequency of the universe is capable of accessing the Universal Akashic Records. However, certain information in the Akashic Records might be "privileged" information in so far as it represents someone's personal history and personal record. This is not to be accessed, except with the permission of the person involved.

Seventy-One

Q: Is there a Great White Brotherhood, or spiritual hierarchy of beings? Describe who these beings are, their work and relationship to humans on earth.

G: Yes. In response to this question I will give a brief outline of the hierarchies existing. Certainly there is a Great White Brotherhood. These are highly evolved souls who work in close cooperation, predominantly from the astral planes, with beings still in existence on this planet. They are very human and very connected to us on all levels. Christ, in the Bible, says, *"In my Father's House there are many mansions"*. And in the cosmos there are many creations, some of which would seem strange to us. The first Great Creation was that of the Angelic species. These beings are free to move between one manifest experience of creation and another. They are the only beings who can cross what might be termed, *intergalactic space*, through the void. All other beings, including earth humans, in order to move from one galactic experience to another must pass through the center of energy, or the heaven center, to move from one manifest universe to another.

Each universe made manifest by the Creator has its own particular form and species inherent to it. The quadrant of the universe in which we are experiencing is predominantly inhabited by the humans. Life is experienced by us through many dimensions within this quadrant. So that there are those of us who have three dimensional density, as we humans on planet earth, and there are also those three dimensional beings of much lighter form than ourselves. And there are equally those on other dimensions who are in pure spirit form alone. All humans are evolving toward the same goal, that of reuniting with the One.

There is the Council of the East Star (or Sirius) which is the ruling body for this quadrant. The members on this council are connected genetically to Sirius, the Pleiades, the House of David and the blood-line of Jesus Christ.

There is another group of beings who usually exist at the *eighth* level but who are currently adopting more density and say they have made a base location in the *third* dimension on Apus, a star in the Southern Hemisphere. They say they are few in number and their work relates to linear time. They are currently involved in the process of introducing more light particles at cellular level into human beings who have so requested.

This small sampling gives you some idea of the variety of entities with whom we are priviledged to share this creation.

SEVENTY-TWO

Q: WHAT IS THE ROLE OF "GOOD AND EVIL" IN THE EVOLUTION OF MANKIND?

G: I don't think they have a role and they are certainly not necessary. The terms "good" and "evil" are judgments. They are definitions that have been placed, as man has evolved, upon the actions of man. We have chosen, through the exercise of our own free will, to embark upon certain actions or undertakings, and then we, ourselves, have determined which of those are "good" and which are "evil". In other words the labels "good and evil" are entirely a product of humans in this human experience and have little or nothing to do with God.

If one wanted to ask, *"What is evil?"* Then I would say this: Remember in the beginning I said that when the Creator created the creation it was then set free, subject to the natural laws, and those are *natural laws of evolution, of movement and of change.* The natural laws require constant movement, constant change, and the pattern of that movement was laid down by the Creator in the laws which He evolved for creation. So you might say that anytime we *exercise our free will* to create a situation *which goes against* those natural laws laid down by the Creator, then that exercise of free will constitutes evil—nothing more and nothing less.

It is interesting to note that the word "evil" is the word "live" spelled backwards. This is a good way of comprehending evil. It is living backwards or living against the flow of the natural laws which were set in motion for the evolution of the whole creation

Evil is that which is out of balance with the universal laws. You could call it *imbalance* because the Creator is perfect balance. The creation is perfect balance. It is only our exercise of free will which causes imbalance at any level. This is from the smallest thing; for example, we have created pesticides and fertilizers to make wheat grow more. "More" meaning more than the Creator ordained wheat to grow. And now the wheat is producing in such a way that the stalks are too weak to hold up the grains. So we now produce another spray for the wheat to strengthen the stalks to hold the grains up so the farmer can cut them. This is imbalance at a very basic level and one can say that this is "evil" because it is against the natural law. At the other extreme you can say that to commit murder is "evil" because the natural law for that victim was that they were going to live a certain amount of time and have a certain experience and someone, by the exercise of their free will, cut that life short. They interfered with the natural process of that person's life. That is an example of "evil". So "evil" is very clearly defined: It is anything, at any level, which goes against that which the Creator ordained. This, of course, raises the question, *"What, exactly did the Creator ordain?"* Perhaps if we knew the answer to that question, we would all be able to agree on what constitutes "good" and "evil".

The presence of evil certainly appears to be increasing during these times of change. When we, as humans, see our security being destroyed around us — loss of jobs, earthquakes, broken relationships — these changes fill us with fear and it is this fear that we are expressing as evil. We are fighting against the evolutionary processes which are occurring at this time, instead of coming to an understanding of them so that they may benefit us and move us forward into the next experience of life. Life itself does not stand still. It is constantly changing and we must learn to change with it. If we can recognize and understand the beauty of those changes which are occurring and the wonders which are being prepared before us, we will no longer fear them. And when our fear is released, so will there be a lessening of the "evil" apparent on the planet today.

SEVENTY-THREE

Q: WILL THE ENERGY BEING CALLED, "SATAN, OR "LUCIFER" HAVE A PLACE IN THE NEXT CREATION?

G: Let me put it this way: The new Creation that man is involving into is not starting out with Satan built into it. Satan (Lucifer), in the Biblical sense, was the first and greatest of God's Angels, the brightest morning star. It was his pride and ego that put him in competition with his Creator and resulted in him becoming tied and trapped by his ego and vanity to this planet. The lesson inherent in this is that we are all tied and trapped to this planet by our pride, our vanity and our egos. Our emotional self-oriented feelings are what tie us to the cycles of reincarnation and hold us back from our spiritual evolution and progress. So long as there are manifest three-dimensional creations, I would think there would also be realistic "Satans" in existence, because they are the expression of the "dark" side of man. They offer temptation and it is the resistance of temptation which serves as a stepping stone to our purpose. It may be that man in his willfullness is incapable of accepting the love of God and giving himself in total abandonment to that God, without first putting himself through the punishment of temptation and the resistance to temptation. If man needs that to grow, then man will have that.

Your Notes

Seventy-Four

Q: Is it true that if one has perfected his soul adequately enough to achieve immorality that he will be somehow targeted by the dark side and attacked in various ways?

G: No this is not true. If one has perfected one's soul and achieved immortality, then one has moved beyond the reaches of this plane and into the realms of light. The "dark" side to which you refer has dominion only upon the earth plane and within the astral realms. It does not have any access to the lighted realms where a perfected soul would be.

However, if you are asking the question and referring to when that perfected soul is still living on this planet in human form, would they be attacked by the "dark" side. We might reasonably say in answer to that, "Yes". The only perfected soul whom I can be sure of is Jesus the Nazarene, since he certainly went into the desert and was tempted and/or attacked by the "devil". I suppose it is because the "devil" never wants to give up and admit that he has lost. Although, of course, he cannot but lose in the end.

Now if one hasn't actually achieved soul perfection, but is working towards it, then one may be tested or tempted by the "dark" side. Perhaps we need to steer away from the focus on the "dark" side and perceive these temptations which are presented before us as a means by which we can evolve our spiritual growth.

There is a Native American saying which goes something like this, *"The best friend a man can have is a powerful enemy."* Because it is through the actions of the enemy that our strength is tested and we move forward. However, it is appropriate in our daily prayers to put emphasis on the line in The Lord's Prayer, *"Deliver us from evil".* For if we have humility, then we know our weaknesses. We know how easily we may succumb to the temptations offered us on this planet. And certainly everything that is presented before us physically, emotionally and mentally represents a temptation with the effect designed to distract us from our sole purpose which is the perfection of our own soul.

Seventy-Five

Q: Is the mark of evil the number 666?

G: No. That is not true. That is a misunderstanding and a manipulation of a reference in the book of Revelation which says the number of a man is 666. The statement is absolutely true. The number of a man, any man, all men, is 666 and refers directly to the fact that there are six electrons in a carbon molecule and that man experiences a carbon based manifest reality in three levels of evolution. We are at the first level of that evolutionary process. Our number is 666 and we have *forty-six* chromosomes. At the next stage of our evolution, our number will be *sixty-six* and we will have *forty-eight* chromosomes. At the next level of our physical evolution, our number will be six and we will have *fifty* chromosomes. When we reach the level of *fifty* chromosome based DNA, our next evolutionary step will be entirely into spirit form. So the 666 is intended to give us understanding of the progress of man as a species as he moves back into his pure spirit form through three stages of physical manifestation.

What is being made clear to us in Revelation 13 is that the "beast" is not some satanic creature from Hades, but a mortal man like the rest of us. More than this, that this man will have great power over natural things and, because he seems able to perform miracles, many will be deceived and follow him. In these times it will serve us well to remember that "satan" may be "clothed as an Angel".

SEVENTY-SIX

Q: HOW CAN ONE BE SURE OF THE SPIRITUAL QUALITY AND INTEGRITY OF CHANNELED INFORMATION COMING TO THEM PERSONALLY OR TO ANOTHER? IS THERE A WAY TO TEST THE BEING AND KNOW IF THEY BELONG TO THE GREAT WHITE BROTHERHOOD?

G: When receiving channeled information, either for yourself or through someone else, keep in mind that this universe is energy and is dependent, for its maintenance, on energy. Therefore, a good rule of thumb is that the more energy the being wastes in words, the less valuable the information. Evolved beings will not waste the energy of the universe using ten words where one will do.

Now as far as ways to test a being as to its affiliation with the lighted brotherhood, the first rule is always that you must identify your source. Whenever any spiritual being comes to speak to you or through you, always ask them to identify themselves. Once you are satisfied with their identification, you may receive the information that they give to you.

In response to the question about whether *they* serve the lighted brotherhood or not, that is not so important as whether *you* serve the light, or not. For if *you* serve the light, you can stand in the shadow of darkness and not be affected by it. It is only if you are vulnerable to the darkness, that the darkness will have access to you. Make sure that you stand in the light, and then it really does not matter who tries to come to speak to you because your own discernment and knowing will prevent you from receiving that which is not appropriate for you.

It is perhaps also worthwhile keeping in mind that just because someone is dead, does not mean that they have access to all knowledge. You may have a very well-meaning, well-intentioned human in the process of evolution who is still living in the astral plane awaiting a new incarnation and who wishes to give you an endless string of information. Do not automatically assume that that information is correct. It may be no more correct than it was in that persons previous incarnation.

Another thing to keep in mind is the danger inherent in all forms of trance-channeling. It was said to me by Spirit that when any being interferes with the lifestream of another, by entering their minds and bodies and channeling directly through, then that being is still tied by their ego to this planet. Therefore that being is not the most highly evolved of beings, although some of their information may be very valid and useful. The most highly evolved beings will not interfere with the lifestream of another, even for a few minutes, in order to pass on information. Rather they will wait until you, the receiver, are perfectly capable of receiving that knowledge within your own awareness in the fully conscious state.

Seventy-Seven

Q: **What do the terms "Spiritual Transmutation", "Ascension" and "Transfiguration" mean?**

G: As we grow spiritually and move towards enlightenment, a literal process of taking more light into the body occurs. This process is known as transmutation of cellular structure in which our bodies themselves undergo change.

Ascension means lifting up to some other plane of experience with our soul holding the pattern of a transmuted body.

Transfiguration is to change the outward form or appearance; to transform. Bearing in mind that your "outward form" is your body, I suggest a close study of St. Mark, Chapter 9 in the New Testament of the Bible. This is truly a teaching for *"Those who have eyes to see".*

Your Notes

SEVENTY-EIGHT

Q: ARE THERE ACTUALLY SPIRITUAL INITIATIONS? AND WHAT ARE THEY?

G: True initiations exist both on the material and on the spiritual planes. From time immemorial man, in his search for spiritual growth and understanding, has evolved rituals and tests to put the neophyte through in order to measure the level of his growth. These vary from the gentle initiations of the little girl at first communion, to the more brutal initiations of the ancient Celtic and Egyptian beliefs, in which a man could easily lose his life in the process.

The spiritual initiations are placed upon us by our spiritual guides and teachers in accordance with our level of spiritual growth. Who determines what these initiations will be, the form they will take, or the fruit they will bear is not known to me.

There is one attribute in common with all initiations, both mundane and spiritual, and that is the commitment of the participant.

SEVENTY-NINE

Q: WHAT DOES IT MEAN TO BE "FORSAKEN" BY GOD? WHY AND WHEN DOES THIS HAPPEN TO AN EVOLVING SOUL?

G: God never forsakes us. However it may be that as the soul is evolving, it goes through a period of time and experience when it is no longer able to find and reach communion with God, or with the spiritual guidance through whom the creative energy has in the past been in the habit of flowing into their souls. This has been referred to in literature as "*The dark night of the soul*", and is indeed a most terrible experience. For in this dark night, one lives in silence without that sense of unity and communion. This is always a major test of faith for the evolving soul. And it may be that their love of God and trust in their Creator is being tested.

Or it may be that they have reached that level of their own development where they are required to fulfill the Biblical adjunct which says, *"When we are children, we play with childish things, and when we are adults we put those childish things away".* So as we become adults, spiritually speaking, we may be called upon to stand upon our own feet, without the conscious daily inflow of knowledge and information from Spirit which has previously sustained us.

During this time the flow of Divine Love into the soul does not cease, but rather, becomes hidden from the conscious awareness. Although this can be a time of great agony to live through, I feel that it is a time when God can work the greatest miracle on a soul which will bind that soul to Him for eternity.

EIGHTY

Q: **PLEASE DISCUSS WHAT BALANCED PARENTING INVOLVES.**

G: The relationship between parents and young children is the one exception which breaks the first two rules of the Universe. This is because the parents have the responsibility directly, by exercising their free-wills, in making judgments and choices *for* their young children. Because of the Karmic implications involved, a wise parent will teach their children at the earliest possible age to choose for themselves and make appropriate decisions, with parental guidance, for themselves. The most essential qualities of parenting which aid in developing the well being of any child are *consistent love* and *consistent discipline*. Without knowing the boundaries of behavior, a small child cannot learn to choose for itself. Those boundaries of behavior and acceptability must be laid down by the parents. And this discipline must be consistent and define all areas within which the child can grow and learn.

EIGHTY-ONE

Q: WILL YOU DESCRIBE WHAT ALL THE CHANGES ARE ABOUT?

G: The winds of change are sweeping through the consciousness of humanity as man and all Creation prepares for the next evolutionary step forward. These changes affect the socioeconomic, political, geophysical and the spiritual environment. The last decade has seen a multitude of books written about government disclosures, terrorism, global economy, survival and so on. And the new age has seen a plethora of new and sometimes strange belief structures arising around the world, as well as, the return to many old belief systems. As we fast approach the end of this cycle, people en masse are beginning to ask themselves the age old questions, *"Who am I? Why am I here? Where am I going"*

With regard to the socioeconomic and political changes, I like to use the analogy of an aircraft which is taking off. As you know, it travels down the runway and for a period of time it is within the province of the pilot to decide not to take the plane off the ground. He can put the brakes on and change the plan. But there comes a point of speed and distance where aborting the takeoff is no longer possible and the plane must leave the ground. When one is looking prophetically at the future events that are socioeconomic and political, one can often see three or four events stretching out in front of us. And after each of the first two events, something occurs which makes it possible for us to change our destiny, to change the path of history. But if the first three events occur, then one can say that the fourth becomes inevitable. Many of the events that we are going to be seeing in the future in this world have now become inevitable. For example, in 1990 when the United States troops entered the Persian Gulf, we had a period of two or three months before the war began. In this two-three month time frame, we had the option to change history, in that we could choose whether to settle our differences by negotiation or by warfare. We chose warfare, and in that choosing, we made the Third World War inevitable.

In the same way there is another matrix of energy approaching in October of 1994 on the timeline of the United States. This is such a huge conflux of energy, that it will have to be used in some major national way. We will have the choice at that time to utilize that energy into social productivity, healthcare reform, job reform, education reform, etc., or we will find ourselves involving our resources in more contentious situations. Undoubtedly we can expect to see war breaking out in many global areas anytime after the beginning of October 1994.

Eighty-Two

Q: WHAT ABOUT THE GEOPHYSICAL CHANGES?

G: As to the geophysical events which are occurring on the planet—
over these we have little or no control. We can only control the way in
which we manage the events, not the events themselves because these
events are fulfilling a natural cycle of the planet itself. As much has
already been written about the earth changes, I do not feel it necessary
to go into them in detail. And I would not disagree with any of the writings
of the well-known seers which are available to us today. However I am
often asked, *"Why is it that one seer gives this date and another gives
a different date, and another says the events will occur in this area, and
another in that area."* If you look at the prophecies overall, you will see
that the general trend is the same.

I think the confusion arises from the use of the word, "shift". There are
two parallel shifts occurring. One still to come, the probability of a polar
shift, which may well occur sometime between 2011 and 2014. And then
there is the shift which is already occurring, and which is not just an earth
event, but also a cosmic event. This is approximately a 21 degree
movement. The first 7 degree movement occurred on October 7, 1991.
This is a movement of our entire quadrant of the universe to realign us
to the central energy source of the universe. When that alignment is
complete, the eastern face of planet Earth at sunrise on the Spring
Solstice will be directly aligned with one of the suns in the Pleiadian
system. That will in turn have aligned us with the Central Sun. Because
everything in our system is measured relative to everything else, when
everything is moving we are not aware of the actual change of our

position. In other words our relative position stays the same. As I said, the polar shift is a probability which may or may not occur. And it is the polar shift which will have the most direct impact, obviously, on the weather changes and on the geophysical events associated only with planet earth. But it is the huge cosmic shift of our quadrant which aligns us to that point where we can make the quantum leap in our evolutionary experience. This shift is already in process of occurring, and will continue. It is indeed an unchangeable aspect of the geophysical events. It will not, however, have any directly obvious effects on the weather patterns, earthquakes and volcanos. But of the two, it is the most important event.

Another factor which is affecting us geophysically is the entry into our system of a planet and its accompanying moon which is making a 3600 year orbital pass through the solar system and is presently out beyond Saturn. It is my understanding that the accompanying moon is approximately 94 percent iron and that in itself causes major alterations in the magnetic fields within our system. In addition to that, there is a very high probability that that accompanying moon will collide with one of the outer moons of Saturn. Should that occur the shock waves felt throughout our system will undoubtedly cause us to experience major tidal effects, earthquakes and volcanic eruptions. Although I am uncertain of the date for this collision, it is possible that it could occur as early as 1998 and it may occur as late as 2014. This event should not be confused with the "big bang" event that science is now talking about with regard to the asteroid particles colliding with the back of Jupiter. This Jupiter/Astroid collision is prophesied for July 18th of 1994. By the time you are reading this book, that event will have already occurred.

Relatively speaking that is a minor event compared to what will happen should the transiting moon and the moon of Saturn collide. In the case of that event, and I quote from Spirit, *"The stars will shine red and because of the wobble created on the earth's orbit, the sun will appear to go backwards at mid-day."* When we see that event occurring, we will have three to four days in which to reach high ground. Because as I said, the first and most hazardous effects will be tidal waves in all coastal areas, with oceans rising 30 feet and higher. It was suggested by Spirit that "high ground" should be understood as 1,200 feet above sea level.

EIGHTY-THREE

Q: TELL US ABOUT THE SPIRITUAL CHANGES.

G: As to the spiritual changes, what we are witnessing now worldwide is a mass awakening into *conscious* awareness. There is a tendency for us to measure our consciousness in scientific terms related to brain waves and the ability to see, smell, hear, taste and feel. And to believe that if we are aware of our five senses we must be conscious. But we do not in actuality become conscious beings until we ignite that Living Spark within our own immortal souls. It is this act of self-awareness, this lighting of the immortal fire within that I refer to when I speak of the rise of consciousness among the millions of people across the face of this globe.

Let me share some words with you that were given by Spirit: *"Thine is the kingdom within the secret chamber at the heart of the spiritual body where burns the Three-Fold Flame of Power, Wisdom and Love. That sacred fire is our eternal link with the Creator. We fuel the flames ourselves. By our choice we add to the brilliance of the flames. Do you fan only the flame of power? Do you look for power in the world and over others? The measure of true personal power is in direct proportion to the integrity of the soul. A wise man seeks to find balance in all areas of growth and draws his inspiration from above rather than from below. For the greatest power is the power of creation. You are the kingdom. And the glory is the love of the Creator shining through you. By your choices you add to the flames. Be sure you fuel your eternal fire with sweet smelling balsams so that your flames may burn brightly within you and your light shine upon all you meet."*

As we have said throughout this book, this eternal spark is the very essence of your soul. And by igniting that spark and adding the fuel of your life to the flames, you create the energy of your immortal soul. You become an immortal living being.

The sacred Three-Fold Flame of Power, Wisdom and Love is the living energy which manifests throughout the universe. Each day we must nurture that sacred flame, the essence of our own soul.

In this matter, Spirit also made the following statement: *"The power is in the burning bush; wisdom. These are the fires which burn, but do not consume. So if you are perfect as your Father in heaven is perfect, then you will be in spiritual harmony with all things and so be given to see, to be aware, of the fire of the burning bush. As all things are in a constant state of growth, creation and recreation, so all things are afire at all times. That which is already pure and innocent changes, but is not consumed. That which is "evil" is consumed and cannot withstand the flames. There is no sentiment in this flame, only cleansing—truth stripped bare. Do not undertake guardianship of the flame lightly, for in truth you are become the keeper of the soul of the world."*

This flame which is the very essence of your soul is the center of your form in any level of manifestation. Let us then look again at the forms on page 3.

In the diagram on the following pages, we offer you some "clues" which can serve as a base with which you can expand your awareness of you, the universe and all the possibilities your immortality has to offer. We hope you will enjoy these puzzles.

As you start tying all these bits together, you see the idea of the original form—the sign wave or vibration. Free in the vast reaches of infinity and in union with the One. And then being segregated into the individually named unit and manifesting for a period in a linear time frame. Now add the concept of the greater and lessor cycles of creation and you begin to get the feel of eternity. And you are an aware, active participant who can choose your own destiny in all of this.

So what do you have to do as you move through these changing times? That, fortunately never changes. You simply have to learn the laws and obey them. This is called spiritual growth and is a path without beginning or end. For in the completion of the circle you simply return to your beginning. And so it begins again, a never ending, ever expanding spiral of knowing. As you climb higher and higher, the air becomes more rarified, the vibration swifter, the tone sweeter and the more you become, the less you are, until at last there is nothing of you left and you are once again a part of the whole. This is a journey of light and light is not *to see* by, but *to be* by. It is the energy for the illumination of the soul.

There are many schools of thought which tell you that this dear planet earth is a lower place of learning at the bottom of the totem pole. But I tell you this: From this place, you can leap frog into heaven if you so choose for there is no place in God's creation which is closed off from direct contact with Him. Now is a time of great challenge and also great opportunity. Stay fixed in your purpose and shine brightly and you will not be overlooked, for *"He will know His own."*

THE COSMIC COMIC STRIP

IN THE BEGINNING THERE IS THE SOURCE.....

AND THE SOURCE EMITTED PARTICLES AND NAMED THEM "PHOTON" (LIGHT).....

AND THE SOURCE BREATHED INTO THE PHOTONS UNTIL EACH CONTAINED IT'S OWN VIBRATION

AND SOME WERE AS TWO 3-SIDED PYRAMIDS, AND THESE MANIFESTED ALL THAT IS IN THE THREE DIMENSIONAL WORLD — BUT TO DO THIS.....

AND THIS IS YOUR ORIGINAL FORM. BUT....

THEY HAD TO ROTATE THEIR UPPER AND LOWER HALVES AT 90° TO ONE ANOTHER

NOW, INTO SOME PHOTONS THE SOURCE IMPARTED THE TOTALITY OF IT'S OWN ESSENCE AND, LIKE A FRAGMENTED MIRROR, EACH CONTAINED THE WHOLE.....

NOW HAS COME THE TIME TO UNDO YOUR 90° OFF-SET AND RETURN TO YOUR ORIGINAL DIAMOND FORM IN ORDER THAT YOU MAY.....

BY MANIFESTING IN 3 DIMENSIONS, YOU ALSO ARE OFF-SET AT 90°

YOUR SPIRAL OF LIFE, YOUR KUNDILINI, IS YOUR ORIGINAL ESSENCE AND ALL THAT YOU HAVE ADDED TO IT.

REVERSE GEARS!

EXPAND TO A 4-SIDED DIAMOND AND THEREBY MANIFEST IN THE 4TH DIMENSION.

THIS REQUIRES A LETTING-GO OF THE TIES TO THE KNOWN WORLD AND A REALIGNMENT OF YOUR SPIRITUAL ENERGY.

PUT YOUR TWO HALVES BACK TOGETHER AS THE TRUE DIAMOND FORM AND YOU WILL "SEE THE LIGHT."

IN ALL MEDITATION TECHNIQUES WE SEE THE PYRAMID OF ENERGY SO:

NOW SEE IT SO:

AND REMEMBER YOUR "UPPER HALF"

EIGHTY-FOUR

Q: CAN THESE GLOBAL CHANGES BE AVOIDED?

G: In accordance with God's Law of One, all that is is part of the Infinite Mind of the Creator. It is however, to man that the gift of thinking, reasoning, and the exercise of free-will is given. Man, may therefore, to a great extent choose the time of his own evolution through his soul's efforts. Whereas the planet, and all other creatures of the cosmos, evolve according to the time frame set down by God within the natural laws He established for the progress of His Creation. As evolution is fundamentally the breakdown of old patterning and the establishing of new patterns, so we will see the breakdown of the known planetary systems in preparation for the emergence of the new world.

EIGHTY-FIVE

Q: WILL YOU EXPLAIN SOME MORE ABOUT WHAT THE SOCIOECONOMIC AND POLITICAL CHANGES ARE ABOUT? MUST THEY OCCUR AND DO THESE CHANGES INCLUDE WHAT IS TERMED AS "THE NEW WORLD ORDER"?

G: Yes. Two thousand years ago a man we know as Jesus of Nazareth was sent to give us a perfect set of rules for living. He was a teacher and fundamental to his teachings was the admonition he gave to all who would be his disciples, *"Love ye one another as I have loved you."* Love as he loved. That is to say, love all equally with honor and respect for the essence of the Creator at the heart of every living soul. If one loved all equally then each person would *"Do unto others as they would be done by"*.

Unfortunately this has not been what has occurred during the past 2000 years. Man has exercised his own free-will to serve his own self-gratification at every turn. So now we are facing the situation where "The New World Order" will be imposed upon us by force, by dictatorship, undoubtedly by means in which will cause many of us, especially the free-thinkers, to not enjoy life or wish to participate in it.

However, when examining the precepts of "The New World Order" closely, they *do* relate to the equality of man, the equal sharing of man, and the idea that all men have basic rights to the benefits of a certain standard of living. The challenge to each of us is that "The New World Order" will be *imposed* upon us. We will be forced to work at any employment which the government demands of us to maintain production and economic stability. We will be forced to give our money in taxes to feed the poor. We will be forced to go and fight wars wherever we are told to go and fight them because somebody decides that something will be more equally shared in a specific way. But nonetheless, we are having imposed upon us, albeit from the dark side, the teachings of Christ which we refused to obey, when given by Him from the good, light and loving side. If we could not obey the request of God, we will obey that request through the demands of man. We will learn to share. We will learn to take care of our brother. We will have it forced upon us, whether we want to or not. So yes, "The New World Order" is a manifestation of the socioeconomic and political changes, and yes, it is absolutely necessary for the evolution of the humans on the planet at this time. This is because humanity as a whole has failed to live in balance on the planet. A famous person once said, "*People get the governments they deserve*". We may not like everything we get, but we do get what we deserve. And if individuals have problems with the more national and global systems which seem to be invading privacy at all levels, it is because that is what we deserve.

In these historic days of change we need to garner all the personal power we can in order to strengthen our resolve to stand *with* God, for before all is finished, we will be tempted many times to ease our load and make our way more comfortable by acquiescing to those who offer the least line of resistance.

The Master, Jesus the Nazarene, gave us the teachings for "right living". We chose not, for the most part, to introduce those concepts into our social and political management of the planet. Now many of those concepts are going to be forced upon us and we will not like it one bit.

If we had learned to love as Christ instructed us, we would have *no* hunger, *no* sick without help, *no* unwanted children or old people. And if through unconditional love, we had created this Eden from our planet, we would not be in a position now, where an elitist group under the guise of the United Nations New World Order, could find themselves able to dictate our very lives. We did this to ourselves and we will have to endure what we have wrought, but even that is another chance for us to learn, to so strengthen our personal power and not give way to that which we know is "wrong". To do that we must endure, but we must endure with love.

EIGHTY-SIX

Q: WOULD THIS REPRESENT A CHASTISEMENT OR JUDGEMENT BY THE CREATOR?

G: Not at all. Right at the beginning we said, when God created Creation He released it to evolve according to the natural laws. The natural law is Karma, the law of Cause and Effect. What you put out is what you get back. What you sow, is what you reap. We have sown for two thousand years greed, fear, selfishness, serving the ego, not serving God. And what we are reaping is a world governed by Politicians with their own interests in mind, who wish to dictate to us on every level of our existence. That is what humanity has reaped as a result of what humanity has sown. God has absolutely nothing to do with it.

EIGHTY-SEVEN

Q: DOES GOD EVER CHASTISE HIS PEOPLE?

G: Yes. God does chastise His people. In general, though, if we look at political or religious history, God chastises those he loves. Chastisement by means of Divine Interference in the lives of individuals or peoples is generally for the purpose of moving them back on to the right track and bringing them back under the umbrella of His Divine Grace. It is not direct interference in the political decisions exercised by the free-will of the people.

A classic and well-known example biblically of a chastisement by God would be the example of Job. When Job was covered with boils he could see nothing that he had done to deserve the state that he was in, he simply looked around and felt he was doing everything right in his life, and yet all these things descended upon him. And one might say that that was the Divine Hand of God interfering in order that he could see his own errors. But through it all he would not deny His God.[2]

If we are aware of where we are in error in our lives, then we are looking at the difficult situations and recognizing them as the effect of a cause which we instigated. Therefore, we are learning by that process. If we are so blind that we can see no cause that we have instigated for our troubles, then it may be God, out of his love for us, who will create an act of difficulty which will bring us "down" and move us into a state of humility from which we can recognize our own errors and begin to make corrections. So the reason for a chastisement by God would always be an exercise of love to help our growth. In much the same way as a parent who rounds up a child and keeps him in his room every night for a week, because he stayed out until midnight and was only ten-years-old. That chastisement of the child is not because the mother is punishing him so much as because she is concerned that he is not safe out on his own at midnight. So one might say that God's chastisement is a means by which Divine Intervention aids us in rethinking our own values.

[2]For those interested, I understand there is a very interesting and thought provoking interpretation of the story of Job in Jewish writings.

EIGHTY-EIGHT

Q: MANY ASK THE QUESTION OF THEMSELVES, "HOW CAN GOD ALLOW SUCH DESTRUCTION ON PLANET EARTH?" WILL YOU ADDRESS THIS ISSUE?

G: Over the years I have often spoken of the coming earth changes and the possibility of great devastation on the planet. In response to the question, *"How can God allow such destruction?"*, I will offer the following from the Bible: *"And he said, 'Go forth and stand upon the mount before the Lord.' And behold, the Lord passed by, and a great and strong wind rent the mountains, and brake in pieces the rocks before the Lord; but the Lord was not in the wind. And after the wind, an earthquake; but the Lord was not in the earthquake. And after the earthquake, a fire; but the Lord was not in the fire. And after the fire, a still small voice."* Can you see? All Creation runs according to the Law of God. Emanating from God's Laws are the Laws of Nature. It is these laws of Nature which govern the seasons, the rising and setting of the sun and moon, and all the cycles of rebirth on the planet. These earth changes of which we speak are the cleansing and rebirthing of our planet and are happening according to a great cycle of nature. No, my child, do not look for the Hand of God in these things, for they are but natural events occurring in fulfillment of His Divine Law. The Creation is created and the Laws set in motion. Now all must abide by them.

Your Notes

Eighty-Nine

Q: Could a miracle save us from these destructive forces?

G: Divine Intervention in the Law is always the preogitive of God, and indeed, He saves us from many a fall by His Grace. But think a moment, what is *really* happening to the planet? Think of the loving Mother you have or may have had. Suppose your dear beloved mother was sick. Her heart was weary from overweight. Her digestion was poor through years of bad eating. Her lungs could no longer take in sufficient clean air because she was choked by pollution. Her life-blood no longer flowed with ease, but was blocked in every conceivable place. Along comes a great healer who explains the severity of your mother's condition and tells you it will be most traumatic to treat and cure her, but she most certainly can be healed. Would you choose to let you mother go through the trauma knowing she would be well and strong again, or would you intervene because you didn't like to participate in such a traumatic experience as your mother would have to go through?

So, would you intervene and stop the healing of the planet? The planet Earth IS your Mother. She gives you food, clothing, shelter and all you need to sustain your life. But she is tired and sick and needs to heal Herself; to spew out from her mighty volcanoes all that causes her innards pain, to bring relief of all her tensions through the rending of great earthquakes, to wash her hair with torrential rain and to rinse her body with the flood waters. And in a short span of years she will be fresh and whole again, ready to receive her children and offer them refuge during the Golden Years.

Ninety

Q: Will you offer some suggestions for preparations we may make for the changes ahead?

G: There are many books available which are written specifically about physical preparations (see "recommended reading" at the back of the book), so I will make this brief. Basically use common sense. You may need to relocate your home, or you may choose to remain where you are. In making your decision, you would want to avoid the most active earthquake and volcanically active areas, areas near the coastlines, areas with a high concentration of nuclear reactors, nuclear waste dump sites and avoid being near chemical companies.

Small towns (fewer than 10,000 people) are preferable to large cities. Look for areas over primordial rock, such as the Great North American Shield, where you can stay high and dry. Ideally making your family as self-sufficient as possible is desirable. For example, acquire a nice plot of land with plenty of clean water to grow your own food, raise animals or whatever. Start storing some basic foods; dehydrated vegetables, grains, dried fruits, beans, maybe some canned items. Be aware that you may not be able to rely upon the normal power sources we are used to now. So this means, unless you can afford a back-up generator, or are able to supply your own solar or water power, refrigeration and electric or gas heat may not be available.

I am aware that some of you do not have the finances to own your own land, or to even move. You can, however, with careful budgeting, begin storing some extra food and water. Or perhaps you may join with another family and pool resources. Use your own imaginations. There is much that one can do without great expense. And most of us can learn to live with less than we think we can. Set your priorities straight. Food and water you will not live long without, that new stereo or car, you can live without. With a little careful planning now, your life will most likely be less disrupted, than if you made no preparations whatsoever.

Ninety-One

Q: Share what you've learned about the "144,000" referred to in Revelation.

G: Contrary to what is interpreted in the Bible about the 144,000, it does not necessarily refer to this time of change we are in, although from a spiritual standpoint......as there are ganglia in the physical body, so there are in the spiritual body. The physical has a nervous system and nerve endings collected in little bundles—these are called nerve "ganglia".

The spiritual body has a "nervous" or energy system throughout and the points where this system collect and pool information are what we know as the chakras; seven within the physical form, and five in the spiritual extension of the body. The seven physical chakras are located at the base of the spine and upwards in positions relevant to the spleen, the solar plexus, the heart, the throat, the third eye and the crown of the head. It is important to understand that in the pursuit of spiritual growth one is not attempting to overcome the activities of any one chakra, but to bring them all into balance and harmony so that each is operation at its optimum rate of vibration in concert with the others. It is when all are vibrating fully and in harmony with each other that the flow of energy throughout the body is brought into proper balance. When this is achieved the subsidiary "ganglia", of which there are 144,000 spaced along the length of the energy lines of flow, will "spark" and, if the balance is maintained, will shine out and show the true luminous body. It is by this luminosity that those of true understanding may be made known and recognized.

It is right and true that the seven physical and five spiritual chakras must be in balance and harmony for the 144,000 lights to be lit and it is proper to work to this end. But further than this, it is to be understood that this balance and harmony is but a forerunner, a preparation for the enlightenment, for when all is balance and harmony throughout the spirit, body and soul, then and only then can the light enter from above. The synchronization of the vibration is a very delicate matter and it should be seen that it is, therefore, necessary to have the balance without as well as within.

NINETY-TWO

Q: WHEN SOMEONE ASKS A BEING WHO IS ACTUALLY LIVING WITHIN GOD'S WILL, WHAT WILL THEIR RESPONSES BE TO THE QUESTION, *"WHO ARE YOU AND WHAT DO YOU DO?"*

G: I think that we have a glowing example of this on the planet today in Mother Theresa of Calcutta. Do you suppose that Mother Theresa said, *"I want to go out and rescue the sick and dying in Calcutta and I will make this my work and my service to God"?* I doubt that very much. I imagine the scenario was more, *"God, I am abandoned to you, use me."* And the next time she went out on the street, she tripped over a homeless person who was dying and she picked that person up, took them home and looked after them and took care of them. After years of doing this she probably thought to herself, *"I guess this is how God is choosing to use me".*

Your Notes

Ninety-Three

Q: WHY IS THERE THIS PROLIFERATION OF CHANNELING OF SO-CALLED "HIGHER BEINGS" BY SO MANY PEOPLE? IS IT TO DISTRACT OR TO EDUCATE? IS IT PART OF THIS "END-TIME" AND THE CHANGES OCCURRING?

G: As the events are the occurring throughout the cosmos and the magnetic fields around the planets are being altered, so the veil between the dimensions is thinning, and more and more people are able to make interdimensional communications and connections. Therefore, more people are bringing us knowledge and information from other beings in other dimensions. This is very appropriate for this time in our history. Although there are some less evolved beings who are simply interfering and trying to distract people on the planet, in general I would say that the information is given on purpose to educate and help us move forward into the next evolutionary step. It is certainly part of the whole evolutionary change which is going on at all levels at this time.

There is something else, however, I would speak of. In the same way that we are moving towards a point of change on the linear time line for our three dimensional creation, where we will be able to shift from the fourth to fifth dimensional experience of living, so also the other dimensions are progressively moving forward. And in the spring of 1991, the window of opportunity between the fifth and sixth dimensions opened. At that time all those highly evolved beings, with whom many humans had been used to communicating, made their evolutionary forward shift. They are now no longer able to contact us from the very next dimension, but from two dimensions beyond. This makes the communication extremely difficult and very infrequent. So, I will say, since May of 1991, few of the great cosmic beings have actually been in touch with people on this planet.

For example, speaking from personal experience, my life-long teacher, Hermes, was one of the beings who moved forward at that time. It is from him that I received both the warning and the information regarding this movement. The two beings most prominently still in contact with humans on this plane are the blessed virgin Mary and Jesus the Nazarene. Jesus the Nazarene is Master of the change of cycles for this galaxy and Mary is ruler of the next evolutionary progression for humanity. For this reason they both are maintaining close and increasing contact with humans on this planet. And it is anticipated that the consciousness of Jesus the Nazarene will be manifest again on planet earth in the Spring of 1995.

Ninety-Four

Q: Describe what the qualities of the next Creation are and where it is in relationship to Earth.

G: Within our universe there is another spiral galaxy in existence. It is my understanding that when the evolutionary moment in linear time occurs, we will have the opportunity to step through the center of that new spiral galaxy and into the new creation. This new creation is under the auspices of the Blessed Virgin Mary. It is in this place that the highly evolved beings we spoke of earlier are already living and preparing as a new place for us. Christ himself said, *"I go before you to prepare a place for you"*. It is this place which is being prepared. It will be another life experience in which we still maintain many of the attributes of the three dimensional form that we have today, only the new form will exist at a more highly developed level of frequency. There is also a new body form associated with the new creation.

My understanding is that once we pass through the center of the spiral galaxy into the new creation, it will take us the equivalent of one to three years in which to evolve the new body form to the "adult" level so that we may fully participate in the new experience. All those who are deemed sufficiently developed spiritually to be of use, will move forward into the new living experience in full consciousness and will be immediately able to participate in the activities of that new creation which will include aiding and assisting the growth of all those of their less evolved brothers and sisters.

For many who pass through into the new Creation, it will as if they are little children again. They will grow within the new dimension. Yet again there will be many millions who are not ready for experiencing the new life form at this time in human history, and who still have need of the three dimensional experience as it exists on earth today. For all those millions of beings, their transportation into the new creation will take the form of DNA storage in preparation for their rebirth and regrowth in the three dimensional reality.

This is not a judgmental matter. It is simply a case that some are ready to move on to the new creation, and some are not yet ready. For those who still need or have chosen to continue with the three dimensional experience as we have today, a new earth will be prepared, as will new homes on other planets in the galaxy.

The Author

Gillian DeArmond came to the United States from England in 1981. She worked for many years as a registered nurse in England, Scotland and Indonesia but was always involved in metaphysics. She was the pupil of Edna Maye, a well-known Yorkshire clairvoyant, and while in Indonesia studied the Buddhist philosophy as well as Chinese numerology, the Tarot and Astrology. Gillian Currently lives in Twin Bridges, Montana.

FREE!

CATALOG

OF RELATED PUBLICATIONS

CALL

(800) 729-4131

OR

WRITE

AMERICA WEST

P. O. BOX 3300
BOZEMAN, MT 59772

QUANTITY DISCOUNTS AVAILABLE

THE TRUTH WILL SET YOU FREE!